VOLUME 1

Written by
The New Song Nashville Pastoral Team

Crowned Image Publishing
Nashville, Tennessee
www.crownedimage.com

New Song Christian Fellowship
Brentwood, Tennessee
www.newsongnashville.com

Disciple's Handbook: Volume 1

Copyright © 2016 New Song Christian Fellowship

All rights reserved. No portion of this book may be reproduced, stored in a retrieval system, or transmitted in any form or by any means—electronic, mechanical, photocopy, recording, scanning, or other—except for brief quotations, without the prior written permission of the publisher.

Published in Nashville, Tennessee, by Crowned Image Publishing.

www.crownedimage.com

Special discounts are available on quantity purchases by corporations, associations, and others. Orders by US trade bookstores and wholesalers—for details, contact the publisher at the website above.

Unless otherwise indicated, all Scripture quotations are taken from The New King James Version (NKJV), copyright © 1979, 1980, 1982, Thomas Nelson, Inc. Used by permission. All rights reserved.

Printed in the United States of America

First Edition, 2016
ISBN: 978-0692693049

Table of Contents

Lesson 1: **Repent**	Page 8
Lesson 2: **Believe**	Page 18
Lesson 3: **Be Baptized**	Page 28
Lesson 4: **Obey**	Page 40
Lesson 5: **Love**	Page 50
Lesson 6: **Worship**	Page 60
Lesson 7: **Pray**	Page 70
Lesson 8: **Forgive**	Page 80
Lesson 9: **Give**	Page 90
Lesson 10: **Serve**	Page 100
Lesson 11: **Preach**	Page 110
Lesson 12: **Abide**	Page 120

Disciple's Handbook
USER GUIDE
Here's How to Use Your Disciple's Handbook

If you are going through this material on your own, just make your way through one lesson at a time. It is recommended to do one lesson per week.

If you are going through this material with a Small Group, here are some guidelines to help you.

<u>Before Small Group Meeting:</u>
1. Read, complete and personally apply Sections 1, 2 and 3 of the current week's lesson in preparation for the upcoming Small Group meeting.
   - To give you ample time and ability to get the most out of this material, it is recommended you do Sections 1, 2 and 3 at different times in the two weeks prior to Small Group.
   - Use the journal pages provided to write your responses.

<u>During Small Group Meeting:</u>
1. Your Small Group Leader will guide you through a review and discussion on how each person in your group is growing as a result of the previous lesson.
2. Your Discipleship Small Group Leader will guide you through a review of Section 1 on what, why & how.
3. Your Discipleship Small Group Leader will guide you through a review and discussion of Sections 2 and 3 (Study and Discussion) with your Discipleship Small Group.
4. Pray as a group about the content of the lesson and it's implementation in your lives.

<u>After Small Group Meeting:</u>
1. Look at the characteristics described in the "Marks of Maturing" section at the end of the lesson. How well do they describe you? Use the journal pages provided to write your responses.
2. Use the optional resources in the "Go Further" section at the end of the lesson to go deeper in your understanding of the lesson topic.

Disciple's Handbook
DISCIPLESHIP SMALL GROUP LEADER GUIDE

If you are leading a Small Group, here are some guidelines to help you.

Before Small Group Meeting:
1. Read, complete and personally apply Sections 1, 2 and 3 of the current week's lesson in preparation for the upcoming Small Group meeting.
   - To give you ample time and ability to get the most out of this material, it is recommended you do Sections 1, 2 and 3 at different times in the two weeks prior to Small Group.
   - Use the journal pages provided to write your responses.
2. Make a connection with each person in your Small Group a few days before Small Group meeting to see how they are doing with the lesson.

During Small Group Meeting (Time Frame: 1 hour):
1. Briefly review and discuss how each person in your group is growing as a result of the previous lesson.
2. Briefly review and discuss Section 1 on what, why & how.
3. Review and discuss each person's responses to Sections 2 and 3 (Study and Discussion).
4. Pray as a group about the content of the lesson and it's implementation in your lives.

After Small Group Meeting:
1. Follow up (phone call, email or in person) with each person in your Small Group within a few days after Small Group meeting to talk further with them about how they are processing the lesson. This will also give you the chance to make yourself available for other questions from, and discussions with, the people in your Small Group as you are building relationship together.
2. Look at the characteristics described in the "Marks of Maturing" section at the end of the lesson. How well do they describe you? Use the journal pages provided to write your responses.
3. Use the optional resources in the "Go Further" section at the end of the lesson to go deeper in your understanding of the lesson topic.

Inductive Bible Study Guidelines

Use this guide to help you get the most from the inductive study found in Section 2 of each lesson.

Using the page provided in Section 2 of each lesson under 'examine,' read and write out word-for-word the selected passage of Scripture. Now read the passage aloud to help you examine the scripture in a focused manner. This will help keep you from skimming familiar passages. Think about every word you are writing down as you follow these guidelines:

1. Key words and phrases. When you read through a passage, look for key words (and their synonyms) and key phrases. Repetition of words and phrases will give a clue as to what the author considered important. You may find it helpful to mark these key words and phrases in some fashion in your Bible.

2. Verb tenses. Verb tenses are very important in understanding a passage. They indicate when an action or event has taken place, is currently taking place or will take place in the future. Understanding verb tenses will often unlock a difficult passage.

3. Connecting words. Connecting words reveal key ideas and relationships. Some examples of connecting words are the words but (introduces contrast), if (introduces condition), because (introduces reason), so/therefore (introduces result), as/like (introduces comparison), just to name a few.

4. Lists of words, phrases or related thoughts. A list might be contained within one verse, cover several verses, or spread throughout a paragraph or chapter. Looking for lists will help you to identify sequences of ideas and progressive thoughts recorded by the author. You will want to determine if the sequence is just a random listing, or if each successive thought builds upon or is dependent upon the preceding one.

5. Challenging statements. Be on the alert for challenging statements made by the author. Look for promises, commands, and warnings. When identifying a promise, look for the condition as well. When you determine what command or warning is given, also consider to whom it is given.

6. Insights to the Godhead. One of the major joys in Bible study is getting to know more about the persons of the Trinity—God the Father, Jesus Christ, and the Holy Spirit. As you study each passage, look for insights into each member of the Godhead and record them in the margin, this exercise will be similar to the lists you learned earlier, but these refer specifically to the Godhead

When you have finished the Examine portion of Section 2, use the **Express** column to write the passage in your own words. Write it out like you're telling a friend about it over a cup of coffee. Don't move on until you can write the passage in your own words. You see, you don't really understand it if you can't tell it to someone else in your own words. And you can't obey Scripture unless you understand it. It's that simple. Sometimes, you might have to stop on a passage for a couple of days and talk it out with the Holy Spirit before you can finish putting it into your own words.

In the **Exercise** column you transition from simply *knowing* God's Word to *obeying* God's Word. Look at each part of the passage. Ask God to reveal things you need to add to your life, take away from your life, or change in your life to obey this passage. Be specific. For example, the passage may say that God created the Earth, but you have to determine what that means in your own life. How does your life change because you believe God created the Earth? What do you need to do differently? What can you do in the next 24 hours to obey this passage? Every time you open God's Word, He invites you into relationship. His invitation is called 'grace,' because you can't do anything to deserve it. However, obedience is how you accept His invitation. God lives with those who obey His Word. (John 14:23-24) When you study God's Word you have a choice: choose to obey Him or choose to disobey Him. It is really that simple. This "exercise" column is your response to God's invitation.

"Repent"	LESSON 1

SECTION 1:

A Story of Repentance

Read II Samuel 12:1-13

A man named David, the most popular king in the history of Israel, had a time in his life and reign when he committed terrible sins. He seduced and committed adultery with another man's wife, named Bathsheba. Afterward, when it was revealed that she had become pregnant, David tried to cover up his sin by arranging for Bathsheba's husband, Uriah, to come home from the battlefield in hopes that he would have sexual relations with his wife. Thus, Uriah would be thought to be the child's father rather than David. But Uriah, a noble, loyal and courageous man, would not even stay under the same roof with Bathsheba because of his devotion to his fellow soldiers still on the battlefield. When his deceptive plan didn't work, David compounded the sin of adultery and deception with that of murder. David gave instructions that Uriah be put on the frontline in battle. Then he was to be deserted, leaving him to be overwhelmed and killed by the enemy. Uriah, one of David's mighty men, an innocent and faithful servant, died in battle. With Uriah dead, David took Bathsheba to be his wife, believing that people would see the child as having been conceived within the bonds of their marriage.

In the midst of this horribly sinful cover-up, God intervened. God loved David too much to allow him to continue on in his sin. David had to be confronted and given an opportunity to confess his sin, repent from the heart and be restored to fellowship with God. God sent the prophet Nathan to expose David's sin by telling him a story about a wealthy man who takes from another man his only valuable possession, a lamb. When David, the shepherd-king, heard this story he was furious, and said that a man who would do such a thing should be killed. Nathan's response to David's outrage was this: "You are the man!" David, deeply convicted of his guilt, confessed his sin and genuinely repented. David's prayer of repentance and restoration is recorded in Psalm 51.

The Definition of Repentance

What is repentance?

> Read Romans 2:4 and II Corinthians 7:9-10

Repentance involves turning away from something and turning towards something else. In your case as a disciple, you turn from sin to God. God's kindness leads you to repentance, but godly sorrow produces repentance. The Holy Spirit, whom God gave you at salvation, is at work in this process as He reveals the truth of the Gospel, your sinful condition, and the need for Jesus' gift of salvation. He convicts you in your heart and draws you to God. Repentance begins upon entering into relationship with Jesus, and should be practiced as a lifestyle to maintain intimacy with Him.

Repent in the Greek Language is *"Metanoeo"* (met-an-o-eh-o), a decision that results in a change of mind, which in turn leads to a change of purpose and action. It also means to think differently afterwards, to reconsider. Genuine repentance is not about having regret due to consequences, but instead involves a true change of heart toward God. It results in a wiser view of the past, present and future.

In order for true transformation to take place, you must acknowledge each wrong thought, word, attitude and action as sin. Repentance is not just a change in your outward actions. It is a heart response that will result in clean undefiled thinking. It is a mindset that honors, reveres, and embraces the truth of the Bible, and the will and the ways of God.

Why do I need to repent?

> Read John 15:1-8

The greatest blessing of the Christian life is not just the restoration of relationship between the believer and God, but in having the privilege of enjoying a moment-by-moment, intimate relationship with Jesus. Un confessed, un-dealt-with sin keeps you from close relationship with Him. It stops your ability to live an effective and fruitful life. Ongoing repentance keeps you clear and clean before God and in a place to enjoy everything that intimate relationship with Him can bring.

How do I repent?

> Read I John 1:6-9

Once you ask the Holy Spirit to point out sin in your life and you have a godly sorrow about this sin, confess and acknowledge to the Lord that it is wrong. Sin comes out of your life from a repentant heart by way of the mouth. You repent with your heart, and you confess with your mouth. True confession is speaking the truth that you sinned in thought, word, attitude or action, and taking full responsibility for it. This allows you to acknowledge the wrongness of the sin that you have partnered with as you turn towards God to receive His life-changing and restoring forgiveness, and the grace not to repeat the sin.

When Jesus was teaching His disciples to pray, He said *when* you pray, this is how you should pray, "Forgive us our debts as we have forgiven our debtors." Repentance is not a one-time act. Repentance should be practiced as a lifestyle that will keep you clean before the Lord, opening the way for more intimate and life-giving relationship with Him.

Take ten minutes, stop and ask the Holy Spirit to show you thoughts, words, attitudes or actions that do not line up with the Bible.

Acknowledge and confess to the Lord each thought, word, attitude and action from your response above as sin. Ask, then receive, His forgiveness for each sin. Use the journal pages provided to write these things down.

Throughout the day, every day, continue in repentance, asking the Holy Spirit to show you sin in your life, and help you turn towards God and His ways.

SECTION 2:

The Study of Repentance

This inductive Bible study will help you respond in obedience to the truth of God's Word. As you look at each passage of Scripture below, *examine* what it says, *express* what it means, and consider how you will *exercise* it in your life. Use the Inductive Bible Study Guidelines and Worksheet provided on the following pages to help you.

Read *I John 1:6-9* and write it down using the journal pages provided.

Read these scriptures aloud and declare your commitment to the truth of them in your life. Use the journal pages provided to rephrase these scriptures in your own words.

Write down 2-3 action steps that you will take based on the truth of *I John 1:6-9*, using the journal pages provided.

Inductive Bible Study Worksheet

Inductive Bible Study Worksheet

Inductive Bible Study Worksheet

SECTION 3:

The Discussion about Repentance

Use the journal pages provided to write your response to each of these questions, in preparation for a group discussion.

 What role does the Holy Spirit play in repentance?

 In your life, what will the fruit of genuine repentance look like? Share a recent example of how this understanding might have led to greater intimacy with Jesus and better relationships with others if you had walked out the steps of repentance.

 How will you cultivate a lifestyle of repentance in your life?

Marks of Maturing

These are the Marks of Maturing as someone who repents. How well do they describe you? Use the journal pages provided to write your response.

- A disciple is someone who receives rapid revelation, and daily lives with openness to the conviction of the Holy Spirit.

- A disciple is someone who has a rapid response to the conviction of the Holy Spirit, and daily confesses their sin with godly sorrow.

- A disciple is someone who chooses rapid repentance, and daily turns away from sin and selfish ways, turning towards God and His ways.

Go Further

Here are some optional readings for you as you walk in repentance:

Repentance is different than regret. In John MacArthur's book, *The Murder of Jesus*, he writes, "Tears of repentance can in no way atone for sins. But genuine sorrow is nonetheless an important sign of true repentance, signifying that a change of mind and heart have truly taken place. Not all sorrow signifies true repentance, however. Judas was remorseful over what he had done and tried to return the blood money to the ruling prisets. His guilt over what he had done finally even motivated him to go out and kill himself. But that kind of sorrow is a worldly sorrow that only leads to death. It may involve sincere remorese over the consequences of one's sin—regret over the loss of prestige or friends or influence. But it reflects no true change of heart, and thus no true grief over the sin itself. Peter's sorrow was of a different sort. It was the deepest possible sorrow of heart—mingled with shame over his sinful behavior, hatred of the sin itself, and a desperate longing to be restored to a right relationship with Christ."[1]

****

"True repentance has a double aspect. It looks upon things past with a weeping eye, and upon the future with a watchful eye." Robert Smith[2]

---

[1] *The Murder of Jesus*, John MacArthur, Nashville: Thomas Nelson 2002.
[2] *www.famous-quotes.com*, Robert Smith

****

Generous in love—God, give grace! Hug in mercy—wipe out my bad record. Scrub away my guilt, soak out my sisns in your laundry. I know how bad I've been; my sins are staring me down.

You're the One I've violated, and you've seen it all, seen the full extent of my evil. You have all the facts before you; whatever you decide about me is fair. I've been out of step with you for a long time, in the wrong since before I was born. What you're after is truth from the inside out. Enter me, then; conceive a new, true life.[3]

---

[3] *The Message Bible*, Psalm 51:1-6

"Believe" LESSON 2

SECTION 1:

A Story of Faith

> Read Romans 4:1-25

"Abraham believed God, and it was accounted to him for righteousness."
Romans 4:3

At 75 years of age, a man named Abram left his country and his family to move to a land that God would show him. God promised to bless Abram and to make him a great nation. He promised to make Abram's name great so that in him all the families of the earth would be blessed.

Though God prospered Abram tremendously, ten years had passed and there was no son. While he had vast riches to pass down, their was no heir to leave them to. In addition, Abram's wife, Sarai, was 75 years old and far past childbearing age. Abram began to wonder how any of this could come to pass. At this time the Lord came to Abram in a vision and said, "Do not be afraid, Abram. I am your shield, your exceedingly great reward." But Abram said, "Lord God, what will You give me, seeing I go childless, and the heir of my house is Eliezer of Damascus?" (Genesis 15:1-2) Then God brought Abram outside and told him to count the stars in the heaven. He promised that Abram's descendants would be more than he could possibly count. Abram believed God. He wholeheartedly trusted in the word of the Lord. God made an oath with Abram to fulfill His promise.

Then, at age 99, Abram encountered God again and fell on his face in reverence and awe. God changed his name from Abram, which means "exalted father," to Abraham, which means "father of a multitude." He reinforced the covenant and the promise of a son.

A year later, Isaac, which means "laughter," was born. Abraham, now 100, and Sarah now 90, were filled with joy and laughter. The miraculous promise Abraham had believed 25 years for had come to pass. He learned that God always moves on behalf of those who believe His word.

The Definition of Believe

What does it mean to believe?

> Read Matthew 9:27-29 and John 9:35-38

Believing involves relying completely on something with unwavering confidence. As a disciple, your conviction that God exists, is the Creator and Ruler of all things, and the Provider and Bestower of eternal salvation through Christ, relies on your belief[4] that He is who He says He is.

"Believe" in the Greek language is *"pistis"* (pē'-stēs), which means "to place confidence in or to trust." Genuine belief is not about simply complying, but instead involves a true conviction of heart. The greatest indicator of what we believe is how behave.

Your daily, intimate relationship with Jesus Christ is the source of your faith. Belief begins with a conviction in your heart, a confession of your mouth, and is demonstrated by your actions. As we live faith-filled lives, our profession of our faith in Jesus Christ and His sufficiency will lead us on an epic adventure where we, like Abraham and Sarah, impact the generations to come.

Why do I need to believe?

> Read Hebrews 11:6 and 1 Thessalonians 2:13

When you don't believe that God is who He says He is and that all that He has spoken concerning you is true, you sin against Him.[5] Your faith "pleases" God. In His infinite goodness and love towards you, He has given you this gift of faith by which you are able to experience intimacy with Him. By faith, you are able to unlock the power and promises of God in your life. When you believe that the sacrifice of Jesus is all that you need to receive the gift of eternal life, you put your faith in who Jesus is and what He has spoken through the Bible and by His Spirit. This belief gives you everything God has for you moment-by-moment to live a life of power, freedom, joy and victory.

---

[4] *www.blueletterbible.org*, Strong's G4102
[5] Romans 14:23

How do I believe?

Romans 10:9-10, 17 and John 20:30-31

Just as when you confessed with your mouth and believed in your heart that Jesus Christ is Lord, you must continue to speak words of faith and believe in your heart that Jesus will continue His work in you. God is moved to compassion by your tears, but He is moved to action by your faith. As you believe solely in Jesus and not in our own abilities, wisdom, strength, possessions or achievements, you will overcome every obstacle because He overcame on the Cross. As you completely depend on and trust in Him alone, your confidence will not be in yourself, but it will be in the person, power and promise of Jesus Christ. The good news is that you have the Word of God in written form. As you read, study, and apply His Word in faith, believing that you will receive what He has promised, you will live a dynamic life.

Take 10 minutes to pray and ask the Lord to show you where you might be operating with a mindset of "wishful thinking" or doubt in your life, rather than biblical faith. "Wishful thinking" and doubt are cousins to unbelief. The twin sins of unbelief and disobedience[6] will keep us from entering in to what the Lord has for us.

Acknowledge each area in your life where true biblical belief is absent. The Word says, "Faith comes by hearing and hearing by the Word of God"[7]. Look at what the Bible says about these areas of life and speak them aloud. Then declare the truth about them. This will build your faith in these areas.

As you go through each day, whenever your mind engages this area of your life, or whenever you find yourself confronted by it, recall what God's Word says about it. Then speak the truth out and move forward, confident that the measure of faith He has given you will be exercised and developed, unto your seeing His victory in your life.

---

[6] Hebrews 3:18-19
[7] Romans 10:17

SECTION 2:
The Study of Belief

This inductive Bible study will help you respond in obedience to the truth of God's Word. As you look at each passage of Scripture below, *examine* what it says, *express* what it means, and consider how you will *exercise* it in your life. Use the Inductive Bible Study Guidelines at the beginning of your handbook and the Worksheet provided on the next page to help you.

 Read *Hebrews 11:3-6* and write it down using the journal pages provided.

 Read these scriptures aloud and declare your commitment to the truth of them in your life. Use the journal pages provided to rewrite these scriptures in your own words.

 Write down 2-3 action steps that you will take based on the truth of *Hebrews 11:3-6* using the journal pages provided.

Inductive Bible Study Worksheet

Inductive Bible Study Worksheet

Inductive Bible Study Worksheet

SECTION 3:

The Discussion about Belief

Use the journal pages provided to write your response to each of these questions, in preparation for a group discussion.

 Where have you seen a victory achieved or a promise received in your life that you know was God moving in response to your faith? (This could include your testimony of salvation.)

 Right now in your life, how are you seeing your faith grow stronger as you overcome obstacles and challenges of doubt and unbelief? Share a recent example.

 What is the Lord calling you to believe Him for in the days ahead? In what ways can you partner in prayer with and receive encouragement from others who walk in faith?

Marks of Maturing

These are the Marks of Maturing as someone who believes. How well do they describe you? Use the journal pages provided to write your response.

- A disciple is someone whose words, actions and lifestyle demonstrate faith in Christ.

- A disciple is someone who lives a life of power, freedom, joy and victory as a result of faith in Christ.

- A disciple is someone who does not rely on personal ability, wisdom, strength, possessions or achievements, but instead believes solely in Jesus as the source.

Go Further

Here are some optional readings for you as you walk in belief:

"Faith is the art of holding on to things your reason has once accepted in spite of your changing moods."[8] ~ *C.S. Lewis (British Scholar and Novelist, 1898-1963)*

****

"Faith is deliberate confidence in the character of God whose ways you may not understand at the time."[9] ~ *Oswald Chambers (Scottish Protestant Christian Minister, Teacher and Author, 1874 – 1917)*

****

"Faith in God constitutes the highest worship, the prime duty, the first obedience, and the foremost sacrifice. Without faith God forfeits His glory, wisdom, truth, and mercy in us. The first duty of man is to believe in God and to honor Him with his faith. Faith is truly the height of wisdom, the right kind of righteousness, the only real religion….Faith says to God: 'I believe what you say.'"[10] ~ *Martin Luther (Priest and Professor of Theology, 1483 – 1546)*

Here we have, I. A definition or description of the grace of faith in two parts. 1. It *is the substance of things hoped for.* Faith and hope go together; and the

---

[8] *www.thinkexist.com*
[9] *www.thinkexist.com*
[10] *www.thinkexist.com*

same things that are the object of our hope are the object of our faith. It is a firm persuasion and expectation that God will perform all that he has promised to us in Christ; and this persuasion is so strong that it gives the soul a kind of possession and present fruition of those things, gives them a subsistence in the soul, by the first-fruits and foretastes of them: so that believers in the exercise of faith *are filled with joy unspeakable and full of glory.* Christ dwells in the soul by faith, and the soul is filled with the fullness of God, as far as his present measure will admit; he experiences a substantial reality in the objects of faith. 2. It is *the evidence of things not seen.* Faith demonstrates to the eye of the mind the reality of those things that cannot be discerned by the eye of the body. Faith is the firm assent of the soul to the divine revelation and every part of it, and sets to its seal that God is true. It is a full approbation of all that God has revealed as holy, just, and good; it helps the soul to make application of all to itself with suitable affections and endeavors; and so it is designed to serve the believer instead of sight, and to be to the soul all that the senses are to the body.[11]

---

[11] *Commentary on Hebrews 11.* Henry, Matthew. Blue Letter Bible. 1 Mar 1996. 19 May 2010

"Be Baptized"   LESSON 3

SECTION 1:

A Story of Baptism

> Read Mark 1:4-8, Acts 2:1-4 and 1 Corinthians 12:13

In the nation of Israel, there had been a four hundred year period where no prophet had spoken. That prophetic silence was shattered with the message and ministry of John the Baptist. John, who came in the manner of Elijah, a prophet of old, came with a message that was powerful and profound. John preached repentance from sin and devotion to God, the coming Messiah-King, and the righteous rule of His kingdom. He called everyone who identified with this message to be baptized in the waters of the Jordan River. Those who responded were letting their hearts and their lives be prepared for the coming King who would usher in a new age of salvation and freedom.

Jesus' disciples were instructed to wait in Jerusalem until they were clothed with spiritual power from heaven. They gathered in the upper room of the home where they were staying. In unity of heart they prayed, worshiped and waited. Ten days later, on the Day of Pentecost, 120 dedicated disciples' faithful waiting was rewarded. They were powerfully baptized and filled with the Holy Spirit's power. A new sound from heaven was heard as they spoke in languages they had never learned.

Rather than remaining in the upper room, they spilled out into the streets to encounter the people. Devout Jews from many different nations were now hearing the awesome and mighty works of God in their very own language. Christ's followers had been baptized with the Holy Spirit as Jesus promised! Peter and the other disciples walked in the boldness and power given to them by the Spirit, and stood to testify of Jesus. The people's response was simple: "What shall we do?" Peter then called them to salvation, to repent and to be baptized in water in the name of Jesus.

Peter and the other disciples baptized about 3,000 people that day. Jesus had given them authority to go and make disciples of all nations, baptizing them in the name of the Father and of the Son and of the Holy Spirit. These new believers were wonderfully saved and baptized into the Body of Christ that great day.

The Definition of Baptism

What is baptism?

> Read 1 Corinthians 12:13, Colossians 2:11-12 and Mark 1:8

There are three baptisms that take place in the life of a believer—the baptism into the Body of Christ, the baptism in water, and the baptism with the Holy Spirit.

"Baptize" in the original language of Greek is *"Baptizo,"* from the root word *"Bapto."* Both of these words mean to overwhelm and cover wholly with a fluid. "Baptize" also means to stain, which is the picture of dyeing a garment from one color to another, being completely changed. It also means, "to wash, immerse, and submerge." It is the idea of complete immersion unto transformation.

When you are baptized into the Body of Christ upon salvation, you are completely immersed into the Body, and you become one with all believers in Christ. Water baptism takes place upon your public profession of faith in Christ, and is an outward expression of the inward work of salvation. Water baptism identifies you as being buried with Christ and raised to walk in newness of life. When you are baptized with the Holy Spirit, you are clothed and filled with His person and power, including the ability to speak in a new spiritual language. This new spiritual language, also known as speaking in "tongues," gives you an increased capacity for praying and praising, as you can now pray and praise beyond your own human ability. Additionally, your life is marked with a new courage, boldness and zeal for leading others to Christ.

Why do I need to be baptized?

> Read Acts 1:8 and Acts 2:38-39

Simply put, you need to be baptized in water because you are commanded in Scripture to be baptized as a sign or act of repentance. As you believe, you act on your new faith and are baptized in water to proclaim that you are His. Baptism in Middle-eastern culture was a common practice when a non-Jew would convert to Judaism. For John the Baptist to call Jews to repent and be baptized signaled that something new was coming to fulfill the Law and the Prophets. So then, the baptism you take part in now is an act of obedience to the Lord and your complete identification with Him.

You need to be baptized with the Holy Spirit because Jesus offers Him as the Spirit of Truth, the Comforter, the One who will empower you to live out your new faith. When you are baptized with the Holy Spirit, He comes upon you and in you in a new and powerful way. Jesus desires for you not only to have the Holy Spirit in you to guide and comfort you, but to empower you to live the life He has called you to live. He not only calls you to a radical life of dynamic devotion to Him, but He empowers you for the life He has called you to.

How do I get baptized?

Read: Matthew 28:18-20, John 14:26 and Acts 8:14-17

The Holy Spirit baptizes you into the Body of Christ the moment you believe in the sufficient sacrifice of the Lord Jesus. His sacrifice was the only remedy for the devastation of sin, certainty of death and eternal separation from God. By the work that Jesus did in His life, death and resurrection, and by the work of the Holy Spirit, we are made one with all believers by faith.

You are baptized in water after you come into faith in Jesus. This means you are immersed in the waters of baptism. Any believer can baptize another, however, God has appointed leaders and pastors in your life to do so, as they are your God-appointed spiritual covering. Immersion in the waters of baptism is the biblical way to declare what the Lord has done and is doing in your life.

Jesus has promised you the baptism with the Holy Spirit so that you would have the same power that raised Christ from the dead to enable you to be His witness wherever you go. You receive the baptism with the Holy Spirit when you ask in faith to receive Him as Jesus promised, and then believe that you have received Him.

 Take 10 minutes to examine how you have responded to the three baptisms discussed in this lesson. Have you been baptized in water? Have you been baptized with the Holy Spirit? Use these questions to guide your reflection:

- Have you taken the next steps of obedience to be baptized in water (Matthew 3:11)?
- Have you been released in a spiritual language (Acts 2:4; 1 Corinthians 14:2)?
- Have you experienced increased courage and boldness (Acts 4:31)?
- Have you experienced the release of power in your life for signs and wonders (Acts 6:3-8)?
- Do you have an evangelistic fervor (Acts 9:17-22)?
- Do you walk in the fruit of the Spirit: love, joy, peace, patience, kindness, goodness, faithfulness, gentleness and self-control (Galatians 5:22-23)?

 Write out the areas from the Examine section that you need to grow in. Does your life exemplify on a daily basis what it means to be baptized in water and to be baptized with the Holy Spirit? Note: If you have not been baptized in water or with the Holy Spirit, ask a leader in your life about being baptized in water, and ask them to lay hands on you to pray that you would be baptized with the Holy Spirit. Pray, believing that you will receive a fresh filling of His Holy Spirit.

 Ask someone who knows you well to answer the following questions: From your perspective, how am I doing in walking in the fruit of the Spirit? In what areas do I need to improve?

SECTION 2:

The Study of Baptism

This inductive Bible study will help you respond in obedience to the truth of God's Word. As you look at each passage of Scripture below, *examine* what it says, *express* what it means, and consider how you will *exercise* it in your life. Use the Inductive Bible Study Guidelines at the beginning of your handbook and the worksheets provided on the next page to help you.

Read *Galatians 5:22-26* and write it down using the worksheets provided.

Read these Scriptures aloud, and declare your commitment to the truth of them in your life. Use the worksheets provided to rewrite these Scriptures in your own words.

Write down two to three action steps that you will take based on the truth of *Galatians 5:22-26* using the worksheets provided.

Inductive Bible Study Worksheet

Inductive Bible Study Worksheet

Inductive Bible Study Worksheet

SECTION 3:

The Discussion about Baptism

Use the journal pages provided to write your response to each of these questions in preparation for a group discussion.

examine — How did your experience of water baptism impact your life? What specific manifestations of the Holy Spirit confirm to you and others that you have been baptized with the Holy Spirit?

express — Share areas that you need to grow in the fullness of the baptism into the Body of Christ, water baptism, and the baptism with the Holy Spirit.

exercise — How will you daily live a life of power through the Holy Spirit in a way that impacts others?

Marks of Maturing

These are the Marks of Maturing as someone who has been baptized with the Holy Spirit. Baptism into the Body of Christ and water baptism bring new life, and the baptism with the Holy Spirit brings power for living. The Holy Spirit is the One who brings transformation unto lasting fruit in your life. You mature as you submit yourself to the work of the Holy Spirit in your life. Are you walking in the fullness of each of the three baptisms discussed in this lesson? Use the journal pages provided to write your response.

- A disciple is someone who has heard these truths, has been water baptized and has received the baptism with the Holy Spirit as the Lord has instructed.

- A disciple is someone who is growing daily in the power (Acts 1:8), the fruit (Galatians 5:22-25) and the gifts (1 Corinthians 12:7-11) of the Holy Spirit.

- A disciple is someone who understands the importance of water baptism and the baptism with the Holy Spirit in other believers' lives. A disciple is able to share and lead someone in the baptism with the Holy Spirit.

Go Further

Here are some optional readings for you as you walk in the obedience of baptism:

"The Holy Spirit is sent to regenerate men, to give them a new nature, a new mind, a new outlook, a new everything. There is no hope apart from that."[1] ~ D. Martyn-Lloyd-Jones

****

"Wise leaders should know that the human heart cannot exist in a vacuum. If Christians are forbidden to enjoy the wine of the Spirit they will turn to the wine of the flesh...Christ died for our hearts and the Holy Spirit wants to come and satisfy them."[2] ~ A.W. Tozer

****

So what do we do? Keep on sinning so God can keep on forgiving? I should hope not! If we've left the country where sin is sovereign, how can we still live in our old house there? Or didn't you realize we packed up and left there for good? That is what happened in baptism. When we went under the water, we left the old country of sin behind; when we came up out of the water, we entered into the new country of grace—a new life in a new land! That's what baptism into the life of Jesus means. When we are lowered into the water, it is like the burial of Jesus; when we are raised up out of the water, it is like the resurrection of Jesus. Our Father raises each of us into a light-filled world so that we can see where we're going in our new grace-sovereign country.[3] ~ Romans 6:1-5

****

---

[1] *Life in the Spirit in Marriage, Home & Work: An Exposition of Ephesians 5:18-6:9;* Grand Rapids: Baker Book House, 1973
[2] *The Works of A.W. Tozer,* http://dailychristianquote.com
[3] *Romans 6:1-5, The Message Bible,* found at http://biblegateway.com

"Just as the person being baptized is saying, 'Lord Jesus Who died for me, I acknowledge You as my Savior,' so let each one say, 'Jesus Who was buried for me, I want to leave behind, in this watery grave of baptism's waters, my sinful practices, my selfishness, all clutching ambitions-all to be left behind. They remain in the tomb, and I want to rise to newness of Your life by the power of Your Spirit!' So baptism is intended to be a moment of our saying, 'I'm dying to my old ways' (doubts, fears, passivity, pride, argumentativeness, rebellion, etc.) and one of declaring our entrance into the new life dimensions of 'burial and resurrection' from the power of our past."[4] ~ Jack Hayford

---

[4] *Grounds for Living, Grand Rapids: Baker Book House, 2001, page 131*

"Obey"   **LESSON 4**

SECTION 1:

A Story of Obedience

Read Numbers 13 and 14

God's people, Israel, had been slaves in Egypt for over 400 years. With a display of mighty signs and wonders worked through the Lord's servant Moses, God delivered them out of Egypt's bitter bondage and into His glorious freedom.

After a year's time of learning God's law and being instructed in how to worship and know God, it was time to go into Canaan, the land God had long ago promised to Abraham's descendants, and take it as a God-given blessing. Everything was in place for God to deliver on His promise and for Israel to receive their possession. God commanded Moses to send 12 men, all leaders, to survey the land, both the obstacles and the opportunities; they were to bring back a faith-filled, courageous report to Moses and the people. Among this group of leaders were two men, Joshua and Caleb. They and the other 10 men found the land as God had described it, a land of rich resources with ample room for all. And while there would be a war to wage and work to do to fully possess the land, the God of divine protection and power would be with them.

But rather than obediently bringing back a good report, 10 of these spies brought back a report filled with fear and unbelief. Now these men were not commanded to form their own view as to whether or not the land could be conquered; God had already promised it would be. They were to simply to believe in God's power and obey His directive. Instead, they rebelled against God and their leader, Moses, and they led the Israelites to do the same. Only Joshua and Caleb believed and obeyed God; they spoke words of faith, courage and conviction. But the people rejected Joshua and Caleb's good report, persuaded that the negative report was true. As a result of their unbelief and disobedience, God deemed the people disqualified to enter the land. Instead, they died in the wilderness over a 40-year period. Only Joshua and Caleb, men of a "different spirit," entered the land of promise and provision because they followed and obeyed the Lord fully.

The Definition of Obedience

What does it mean to obey?

> Read 1 John 2:3-6

To "obey" means to follow a command or guidance of another, or to conform or comply with the directives of another. Just as the practice of obedience is critical to the success and safety of a military unit, obeying the commands of the Lord is critical to the safety and success of His entire people. However, understanding the full meaning of obedience is more than just outward actions or behavior. It engages your heart and mind. God says that what He had in His mind for you, from the beginning, is that your life would be patterned after the image of His son Jesus.[4]

"Obey" in the original Greek language is the word "*Hupakouo*," which means to listen to something, hearken, give heed to and follow. It is the manifestation of one's faith in doing what is commanded in the Bible and denotes a continuous submission to the will of God. To obey is two-fold: it is both to hear the Lord *and* to do what He is asking you to do.

In the middle ages, a Latin word that came from the root word "obey" is the word "obeisance." This was used to describe a posture of humility and an attitude of the heart that a common person would render to a king. "Obeisance" was closely associated with the concept of worship. You do not merely obey what the Lord says in your actions, but you intentionally conform your thinking to His way, in your mind, rendering your heart humbly before Him because of who He is.

To "obey" is to follow the commands and guidance of the Lord in your heart, mind and actions, so that He is seen through your life.

Why do I need to obey?

> Read John 15:9-17

Obedience enables you to abide in the Lord's love. When you keep His commandments, He responds by giving you His grace to do what He has commanded. As you are obedient, you will experience more of His manifest presence in your life, and have a more intimate relationship with Him. The goal of a disciple is not just knowing about the Father, but looking, sounding and acting

---

[4] Romans 8:29

like the Father in every way. The way you do this is by obeying the things He has told you to do, adhering to the truth of the Bible and guidance of the Holy Spirit, presenting your heart to Him. This produces the life of Christ in you in greater measure. Your obedience enables you to become the person God has designed you to be. Through your obedience, you will bring great glory to God, the greatest good to man, and see the Kingdom of God grow.

How do I obey?

Read John 14:23-24 and Philippians 2:8

The first step in obedience is listening with open ears and an open heart, ready to obey. In Hebrews 13:17 the word submission can be translated as "being softened towards", the idea that you are receptive to "who" is asking and "what" they are asking you to do. Obedience is marked by a rapid response that leaves nothing undone and does nothing different from the orders given. Your response must be one of faith that you are doing the Father's will and His authority and power are with you to do all that He intends. You say "yes" with your heart, set your mind on His will being done, and move in faith to act upon what He has told you.

The Lord helps you to obey through His gift of the Holy Spirit who leads and guides you into all truth,[5] and His written word, the Bible. Additionally, He has placed other believers in your life to disciple, mentor and coach you as you discern His will and obey Him.

examine — Take 10 minutes to examine how you have responded to the Lord in obedience this week. Ask Him by the leading of the Holy Spirit and the truths in the Bible to show you where you have not been walking in complete obedience to those things that He has commanded you to do.

express — Use the journal pages provided to write out the areas from the Examine section that you need to grow in. Write down a prayer acknowledging to the Lord where your obedience has fallen short of His direction. Read it aloud and receive His complete forgiveness for any area of partial obedience or disobedience.

---

[5] John 14:26

exercise — Begin each day by coming before the Lord in worship, or "obeisance." Ask Him to give you specific instructions for your day. In faith, move forward each day, paying attention to the areas you wrote and prayed about above.

SECTION 2:

The Study of Obedience

This inductive Bible study will help you respond in obedience to the truth of God's Word. As you look at each passage of Scripture below, *examine* what it says, *express* what it means, and consider how you will *exercise* it in your life. Use the Inductive Bible Study Guidelines at the beginning of your handbook and the worksheets provided on the next pages to help you.

examine — Read *John 14:23-26*, and write it down using the journal pages provided.

express — Read these scriptures aloud and declare your commitment to the truth of them in your life. Use the worksheets provided to rewrite these scriptures in your own words.

exercise — Write down 2-3 action steps that you will take based on the truth of *John 14:23-26* using the journal pages provided.

Inductive Bible Study Worksheet

Inductive Bible Study Worksheet

Inductive Bible Study Worksheet

SECTION 3:

The Discussion about Obedience

Use the journal pages provided to write your response to each of these questions in preparation for a group discussion.

examine — Ask the Holy Spirit to speak to you now about a specific area of your life where you have not obeyed or have partially obeyed. What is that area? How will you repent and fully obey in this area?

express — Share with the group a time where you fully walked in obedience to the Lord. How did it feel? How was it difficult? No matter the outcome, the disciple obeys. God rewards a life of obedience.

exercise — Commit to the Lord that you will obey Him when you hear His voice and read His Word, the Bible. What are the action steps of obedience you will take?

Marks of Maturing

These are the Marks of Maturing as someone who obeys. How well do they describe you? Use the journal pages provided to write your response.

- A disciple is someone whose life is patterned after the life of Jesus.
- A disciple is someone who experiences the Lord's manifest presence in his/her life, and has an intimate relationship with Him.
- A disciple is someone who says "yes" with his/her heart, sets his/her mind on God's will being done, and moves in faith to act upon what He has said.

Go Further

Here are some optional readings for you as you walk in obedience:

"The cross is laid on every Christian. It begins with the call to abandon the attachments of this world. It is that dying of the old man which is the result of his encounter with Christ. As we embark upon discipleship we surrender ourselves to Christ in union with His death... we give over our lives to death. Since this happens at the beginning of the Christian life, the cross can never be merely a tragic ending to an otherwise happy religious life. When Christ calls a man, He bids him come and die. It may be a death like that of the first disciples who had to leave home and work to follow Him, or it may be a death like Luther's, who had to leave the monastery and go out into the world. But it is the same death every time... death in Jesus Christ, the death of the old man at His call. That is why the rich young man was so loath to follow Jesus, for the cost of his following was the death of his will. In fact, every command of Jesus is a call to die, with all our affections and lusts. But we do not want to die, and therefore Jesus Christ and His call are necessarily our death and our life." Dietrich Bonhoeffer[6]

"The natural people – those whose minds have not been enlightened by the Holy Spirit – scoff at us. What we do doesn't always seem logical to them. But then, who says our actions have to be logical? The Bible tells us the natural or carnal mind doesn't understand spiritual things (see 1 Corinthians 2:14). Too often, we

---

[6] *www.christianquotes.org*, Dietrich Bonhoeffer - German Lutheran Pastor/Theologian, 1906-1945

push aside thoughts, saying, 'This doesn't make sense,' and we actually ignore divine guidance. It's true of course, the devil can flood our minds with wild thoughts that we do need to ignore, but if we pray and open ourselves to the Spirit, we soon know the difference. This is an important principle of obedience we must grasp: obeying instead of reasoning, or as one of my friends calls it, 'The Nevertheless Principle.' She says sometimes she feels God leading her to do things that don't always make a lot of sense. When she hears herself expressing that sentiment, she quickly adds, 'Nevertheless.' Then she obeys. That is really all God asks of us: to obey instead of reasoning against something He is telling us to do. The best policy is to check with your spirit and see if you have peace rather than checking with your mind to see if what God is asking is reasonable." Joyce Meyer[7]

"Just as a servant knows that he must first obey his master in all things, so the surrender to an implicit and unquestionable obedience must become the essential characteristic of our lives." Andrew Murray[8]

"Wicked men obey from fear; good men, from love."
Augustine[8]

---

[7] *Start Your New Life Today*, pages 118-119, FaithWords Hachette Group USA New York, NY, February 2008
[8] *www.christianquotes.org*

"Love"

LESSON 5

SECTION 1:

A Story of Love

Read Luke 10:25-37

A certain expert in Jewish law came to Jesus and asked Him a big question: "Teacher, what shall I do to inherit eternal life?" Jesus responded by asking him what his understanding of the essence of the law was. His response was that one should love God with all his heart, mind, soul and strength, and love his neighbor as himself. Jesus answered him by saying, "You have answered rightly; do *this* and you will live." By *"this,"* He meant that he would live a life that pleased God and one day inherit eternal life with God in heaven.

This Jewish lawyer, wanting to know the least he would have to do to be considered righteous, asked, "Who is my neighbor?" Or, in other words, "Who are the fewest people I would have to show love to in order to demonstrate my love for God and be right with Him?" This man was far from understanding what it meant to truly love God and others. Jesus had to find a way to help him see that God's love was to be extended to everyone everywhere.

Jesus proceeded to tell him a story about a Jewish man who, while traveling from the city of Jerusalem to the city of Jericho, was accosted, robbed and beaten almost to the point of death. A Jewish priest traveling the same road saw the unconscious man and chose to pass by on the other side of the road. Another Jewish man looked the situation over and passed him by as well. Then a Samaritan man came upon this life-threatening situation. Samaritans were considered to be carnal and compromising in religious matters, and Jews would have nothing to do with them. Yet this Samaritan man, seeing someone in dire need, had compassion and showed love and kindness to this beaten and bloodied Jewish man. He didn't view the man from a point of race, rank or relation, but rather need and necessity. He used everything that he had to tend to this man's wounds. He used wine to disinfect, oil to soothe, his blanket to bandage, and his donkey to transport the man to a place of rest and recovery. Once at this inn, the Samaritan took care of him and paid all the expenses for his stay and additional care.

Jesus then asked this Jewish lawyer the big question: "So which of these three do you think was neighbor to him?" Jesus made the point clear that "loving your neighbor" means doing whatever it takes to compassionately meet the needs of others.

The Definition of Love

What is Love?

Read Mark 12:30-31 and 1 Corinthians 13:4-8

Love is from God, for God is love.[1] God's love is eternal, unconditional, selfless, unchanging and righteous. Love as God intended it is the highest and purest form of love, which surpasses mere human affection.

The Bible uses three Greek words to describe the English word for "love." *"Phileo"* is the love between friends or brothers; *"eros"* is the passionate, romantic love which is to be shared by a husband and wife; and *"agape"* is the highest form of love. *"Agape"* love was best exemplified by the Father's love for the world when He sent His Son to die, and in turn, the Son's love for the Father and us in that He gave Himself for all mankind. Love does whatever it takes for as long as it takes.

Why do I Need to Love?

Read John 3:16 and 1 John 4:7-11

You are called to love God because He first loved you. He created you as His own special treasure. He did not create you to be robotic in nature, but rather with a capacity to choose. God desires intimate fellowship with you. In order for you to fully experience that intimate fellowship you must have the love of God in you through the person and presence of Jesus Christ. Without this love you are unable to convey God's heart for people.

1 John gives the description of how to know that you are abiding in Christ. If you obey His commands and if you love one another as He has commanded, then you will know Him. You need to love others because Jesus commanded you to and it shows that you truly love God. God's love compels you to love others as He first loved you.

How do I Love?

Read John 13:34, John 15:12-14 and Galatians 5:13-14

Your capacity to walk in a love that is patient, kind, humble, selfless, hopeful and enduring, increases as you walk intimately with God. You love Him with your

---

[1] 1 John 4:8

whole heart, soul, mind and strength. In other words, you love Him with all that you are, putting Him first, seeking Him in all things and pleasing Him only. As Jesus said, "The Son can do nothing of Himself, but what He sees the Father do." (John 5:19). Jesus was intimately connected to the Father because He loved the Father in this way, doing what the Father commanded and did. This will fill you with the love of God. Now you can love as He has called you to love.

Now that you have the basis for what love is, and as you are filled with and experience His love, God calls you to love your neighbor as yourself. In fact, the Bible says that the greatest expression of love is to lay down your life for another. Your love and intimacy with Jesus will grow as you follow His example in loving others in this way.

examine — Take 10 Minutes to examine what you have learned about love, how you are to love and why you are to love. How are you operating in love on a daily basis towards those around you? Ask the Holy Spirit for deeper revelation on how to receive God's love and how to express it to others.

express — Share with the group what your understanding of love has been, including if you have had any misconceptions about love and what it really is. Share how you will live out a life of love towards God and others.

exercise — Take what you have learned about love and put into practice what you now know about love as you ask the Spirit to show you how to love each person you encounter. Start with your family or closest friends.

SECTION 2:

The Study of Love

This inductive Bible study will help you respond in obedience to the truth of God's Word. As you look at each passage of Scripture below, *examine* what it says, *express* what it means, and consider how you will *exercise* it in your life. Use the Inductive Bible Study Guidelines at the beginning of your handbook and the worksheets provided on the next pages to help you.

examine — Read *1 John 4:7-11*, and write it down using the worksheet provided on the next page.

express — Read these scriptures aloud and declare your commitment to the truth of them in your life. Use the worksheet provided on the next page to rewrite these scriptures in your own words.

exercise — Write down 2-3 action steps that you will take based on the truth of *1 John 4:7-11* using the worksheet provided on the next page.

Inductive Bible Study Worksheet

Inductive Bible Study Worksheet

Inductive Bible Study Worksheet

SECTION 3:

The Discussion about Love

Use the journal pages provided to write your response to each of these questions in preparation for a group discussion.

examine — Ask the Holy Spirit to reveal to you specific areas where you allowed the ways of the world to keep you from loving the Lord with all your heart, soul, mind and strength? What are those areas? What steps do you need to take in order to fully love the Lord with all your heart, soul, mind and strength?

express — Share with the group a time where you have experienced God's love through another person. How did it impact you? Now share with the group a time where you were able to express God's love to another person. How did that impact you? Ask the Holy Spirit to show you someone right now that needs to experience God's love through you and write their name down using the journal pages provided.

exercise — Commit to the Lord that you will obey His commandment to love Him and others. What are the action steps you need to take to walk in obedience to loving the Lord and loving others?

Marks of Maturing

These are the Marks of Maturing as someone who loves. How well do they describe you? Use the journal pages provided to write your response.

- A disciple is someone who daily receives love from the Father, and expresses love to the Father and to others.

- A disciple is someone who daily walks with the love of Jesus expressed in heart, soul, mind and strength.

- A disciple is someone who daily demonstrates an understanding of love by loving all in every situation.

Go Further

Here are some optional readings for you as you walk in love:

The Way of Love

If I speak with human eloquence and angelic ecstasy but don't love, I'm nothing but the creaking of a rusty gate. If I speak God's Word with power, revealing all his mysteries and making everything plain as day, and if I have faith that says to a mountain, "Jump," and it jumps, but I don't love, I'm nothing. If I give everything I own to the poor and even go to the stake to be burned as a martyr, but I don't love, I've gotten nowhere. So, no matter what I say, what I believe, and what I do, I'm bankrupt without love. Love never gives up. Love cares more for others than for self. Love doesn't want what it doesn't have. Love doesn't strut, doesn't have a swelled head, doesn't force itself on others, isn't always "me first," doesn't fly off the handle, doesn't keep score of the sins of others, doesn't revel when others grovel, takes pleasure in the flowering of truth, puts up with anything, trusts God always, always looks for the best, never looks back, but keeps going to the end. Love never dies. Inspired speech will be over some day; praying in tongues will end; understanding will reach its limit. We know only a portion of the truth, and what we say about God is always incomplete. But when the Complete arrives, our incompletes will be canceled. When I was an infant at my mother's breast, I gurgled and cooed like any infant. When I grew up, I left those infant ways for good. We don't yet see things clearly. We're squinting in a fog, peering through a mist. But it won't be long before the weather clears and the sun shines bright! We'll see it all then, see it all as clearly as God sees us, knowing him directly just as he knows us! But for right now, until that completeness, we have three things to do to lead us toward that consummation: Trust steadily in God, hope unswervingly, love extravagantly. And the best of the three is love.[2]

*****

Divine love in the Greek language refers to a love that wholly sacrifices itself for the object of its love, realizing the precious value of it. For example, man and woman betrayed God and fell into deep sin resulting in an abominable life, which ultimately led to eternal destruction. In spite of this betrayal, God lovingly sacrificed Himself on Calvary to save mankind. Why? Because each individual soul is priceless to Him. This is divine love![3]

*****

"Love is kindled in a flame, and ardency is its life. Flame is the air which true Christian experience breathes. It feeds on fire; it can withstand anything rather than a feeble flame; but when the surrounding atmosphere is frigid or lukewarm, it dies, chilled and starved to its vitals." ~ E.M. Bounds[4]

"Go forth today, by the help of God's Spirit, vowing and declaring that in life---come poverty, come wealth, in death---come pain or come what may, you are and ever must be the Lord's. For this is written on your heart, 'We love Him because He first loved us.'" ~ Charles H. Spurgeon[5]

"To love is to be vulnerable." ~ C.S. Lewis[6]

---

[2] *The Message Bible*, 1 Corinthians 13:1-13
[3] *The Holy Spirit My Senior Partner*, David Yonggu Cho, Charisma House, Lake Mary, FL 1989, p.12
[4] *www.christianquotes.com*, Edward McKendree Bounds, Clergyman and Author, 1835-1913
[5] *www.christianquotes.com*, Charles H. Spurgeon, Baptist Pastor, 1834 - 1992
[6] *www.christianquotes.com*, Clive Staples Lewis, Novelist/Christian Apologist, 1898 1963

"Worship"

LESSON 6

SECTION 1:

A Story of Worship

Read John 4:1-26

Having recently begun His public ministry, Jesus was traveling north from the Roman province of Judea to Galilee. Between Judea and Galilee was the province of Samaria. While some Jews on this journey would go around Samaria to avoid contact with the hated Samaritans, Jesus, knowing it was the most direct route, went straight through. Jesus clearly did not share whatever bias other Jews had against the Samaritans. Additionally, it appears that God the Father had arranged a "divine appointment" with a certain Samaritan woman desperately in need of an encounter with the Messiah, Jesus. It was at Jacob's well, a familiar Jewish historical site, that Jesus would meet this woman and present His first teaching on worship.

After requesting water from her at the well, a conversation ensued concerning the "living water" of salvation that would perpetually satisfy the "thirst" of the human soul. Then, Jesus proceeded to prophetically expose the sinful brokenness of this woman's life—not to condemn her, but to save her. Perceiving that she was in the presence of a true man of God, and perhaps recognizing her sinful condition, she asked what place one should go to truly worship God and offer sacrifices that would please Him. Jesus explained to her that the time had come where worship was not about a place, but rather a Person, not about a sacrifice, but rather salvation through faith in God's Messiah. He told her that true worshipers would worship in "spirit," spiritually joined to God by the Holy Spirit, and in "truth," worshiping the true God through the true Messiah, and according to the truth of His Word and the sincerity of their hearts. She responded that she was confident that God's anointed Savior was coming, and that He would explain everything concerning how to relate rightly to God. Jesus said to her, "I who speak to you am He."

What Jesus told the Samaritan woman is true for us today: we must worship God in spirit and in truth. We must learn what it means to daily come to a loving and holy God, offering up the sacrifices of passionate praise and intimate, loving worship. We must learn to worship God not as an event but as a lifestyle.

The Definition of Worship

What is worship?

Read Romans 12:1-2 and 1 Chronicles 16:29

To "worship" is to regard with great or extravagant respect, honor or devotion.[1] You were created by God to worship. A life of worship is a life completely submitted to God. Worship agrees with the worth and value of who God is and acknowledges all that He has done for you. Worship is a complete surrender of yourself—your heart, your mind and your actions.

To "worship" in the original Greek language is the word "*proskuneo*," which means to kiss, to fawn, to crouch, to prostrate oneself in homage or in reverence, to adore, and to worship. This is where the English word "prostrate" is derived. You are called to literally lay your life down before the Lord in worship in everything that you do. He calls you to put Him first in your life and seek Him first in all you do.

Worship springs out of a longing to intimately know God and to abide in His presence. It involves faithfully seeking Him, humbling yourself before Him, and recognizing Him as the only worthy object of your worship. Worship opens your heart to the love of God and opens your life to the service of God.

Why do I worship the Lord?

Read Luke 4:5-8 and Psalm 29:2

You worship God because of who He is. Worshiping God reflects your thankfulness for the saving work of Jesus Christ in your life, as well as affirms and demonstrates your relationship with God. Being in relationship with God then produces intimacy with Him, which allows His life to be fully manifest in your life. Your worship invites the presence of the Holy Spirit to guide and direct you during every moment of your day.

When you worship, you are transformed into His likeness. As you meditate on who God is, you become more and more like Him. As you abide in His presence His power flows through you to minister to others.

---

[1] *Merriam-Webster Online Dictionary.* 2010. www.merriam-webster.com

How do I worship the Lord?

Read Psalm 66:1-4 and John 4:23-24

You are called to worship God in spirit and in truth. To worship in spirit requires you to have a right perspective, a right heart, and a right understanding of worship and, more importantly, the object of your worship. When you worship, your heart, mind and actions are fully focused on God, the object of your worship. You are not distracted from, hurried in, or deterred from your devotion to Him. You choose to sit at the feet of Jesus and grow in daily intimacy with Him. As you worship, you pray prayers of thanksgiving and sing songs of praise with gratitude in your heart towards God. As you serve others with this attitude, God sees your service as worship, and it is pleasing to Him.

To worship God in truth, you must be in agreement and union with His Word. Receiving and honoring the truth of His Word, obeying its commands, and meditating on it are acts of worship. You worship God in truth when you live a life of holiness and purity, remembering Jesus' sacrifice on the cross. To worship God in truth is to agree with His Word, His will, and His way.

examine — Take 10 minutes to examine how you have responded to the Lord in worship this week. Ask Him, by the leading of the Holy Spirit, to show you where you have not been completely surrendered to worshiping Him in your heart, your mind and your actions.

express — Use the journal pages provided to write out the areas from the Examine section that you need to grow in. Then begin to worship the Lord aloud in prayer and song.

exercise — Begin each day by coming before the Lord in worship. Spend time praying prayers of thanksgiving and singing songs of praise. Ask the Lord to show you how you can worship Him in your heart, your mind and your actions today.

SECTION 2:

The Study of Worship

This inductive Bible study will help you respond in obedience to the truth of God's Word. As you look at each passage of Scripture below, *examine* what it says, *express* what it means, and consider how you will *exercise* it in your life. Use the Inductive Bible Study Guidelines at the beginning of your handbook and the worksheets provided on the next pages to help you.

examine — Read *John 4:23-24*, and write it down using the journal pages provided.

express — Read these scriptures aloud and declare your commitment to the truth of them in your life. Use the worksheets provided to rewrite these scriptures in your own words.

exercise — Write down 2-3 action steps that you will take based on the truth of *John 4:23-24* using the journal pages provided.

Inductive Bible Study Worksheet

Inductive Bible Study Worksheet

Inductive Bible Study Worksheet

SECTION 3:

The Discussion about Worship

Use the journal pages provided to write your response to each of these questions in preparation for a group discussion.

examine — What does a lifestyle of worship look like in your life? Share with the group the areas you find most challenging as you worship with your heart, your mind and your actions.

express — What is the fruit of a worship lifestyle? Share an example from your life where you have witnessed this fruit as a result of your worship lifestyle.

exercise — What are the steps you will take to cultivate a lifestyle of worship, particularly in the areas you find challenging?

Marks of Maturing

These are the Marks of Maturing as someone who lives a life of worship. How well do they describe you? Use the journal pages provided to write your response.

- A disciple is someone whose life is completely surrendered to the Lord in heart, mind and action.

- A disciple is someone who continues to become more and more like God as a result of a lifestyle of worship.

- A disciple is someone who worships in truth, agreeing with God's Word, will and way.

Go Further

Here are some optional readings for you as you live a lifestyle of worship:

There is a kind of worshipper who "always trusts, always hopes, always perseveres" (1 Corinthians 13:7), and who gets through the storms of life with a heart still blazing. Sometimes it comes down to a simple choice. We may be hard-pressed on every side, weary and not able to sense God. But then a choice faces us—to fix our eyes on the circumstances or cling to God and choose to worship Him, even when it hurts. The heart of God loves the offerings of a persevering worshipper. Though overwhelmed by many troubles, they are even more overwhelmed by the beauty of God.[2]

****

Worship brings ever deepening and expanding dimensions of God-at-work in our world. Worship, in a very real sense of the word, opens a doorway to the power of His presence, confounding dark powers and overthrowing sin's destructive operations. In Paul's words of expressed spiritual warfare, worship and praise exalt God and cast down those facts and forces that seek to exalt themselves above Him. Essentially, it is God's presence—the raw dynamic of His Being and

---

[2] *The Unquenchable Worshipper*, Matt Redman, Regal Books from Gospel Light, Ventura, CA 2001, p.24

Person stepping into a setting-that gives place to His transforming, redeeming, delivering power.[3]

Worship is the believer's response of all that he is--mind, emotions, will, and body--to all that God is and says and does. This response has its [spiritual] side in subjective experience, and its practical side in objective obedience to God's revealed truth. It is a loving response that is balanced by the fear of the Lord, and it is a deepening response as the believer comes to know God better.[3]

****

"The most valuable thing the Psalms do for me is to express the same delight in God which made David dance." ~ C.S. Lewis[5]

****

"As worship begins in holy expectancy, it ends in holy obedience. Holy obedience saves worship from becoming an opiate, an escape from the pressing needs of modern life." ~ Richard Foster[5]

---

[3] *The Reward of Worship*, Jack Hayford, Chosen Books, Grand Rapids, MI 2005, p.27
[4] *Real Worship*, Warren Wiersbe, Oliver Nelson, Nashville, TN 1986, p.27
[5] *www.experiencingworship.com*, 'Great Quotes on Worship'

"Pray"

LESSON 7

SECTION 1:

A Story of Prayer

Read Acts 4:23-31

Peter and John, two of Jesus' disciples, were arrested and brought before Jewish religious leaders to give an account for preaching and ministering healing in the name of Jesus of Nazareth. To these religious leaders, Jesus was viewed as a false teacher and an enemy of the Jewish faith. They believed that any who followed His teachings had to be stopped from spreading dangerous "error" and upsetting the masses. They interrogated these men, trying to intimidate them, frighten them and get them to back down. It didn't work. Peter and John, filled with the wisdom and power of the Holy Spirit, stood strong. However, the threats to do whatever it took to stop them stood as well.

Returning to their fellow believers in Christ, they reported the threats of attack and violence on them. When their companions heard this, they immediately began to pray. They prayed jointly with passion and faith. They prayed that God would grant Peter and John a new level of courage and boldness to continue to speak and act in the name of Jesus. They prayed prophetically as they invoked the biblical prediction that resistance to the works and words of Christ was imminent and needed to be overcome. They prayed that God would move in might and power, producing signs and wonders that would be compelling evidence that Jesus was the Christ, the Savior of mankind.

After they finished praying, the place where they gathered to pray was shaken as though in the grips of an earthquake. Everyone—Peter, John and their comrades—was filled freshly and newly with the Holy Spirit. They now had an increased spiritual capacity to answer to the demands of a new level of ministry activity and challenges, both human and demonic. They went out from that place preaching the Gospel and demonstrating its power with Holy Spirit-provided boldness.

What made the difference here was a people committed to pray to God to act according to His Word and will. When we pray to God in faith and total dependence, He answers and acts in might and power.

The Definition of Prayer

What is prayer?

> Read Philippians 4:6-7, Ephesians 6:18, Romans 8:26-28

Prayer involves listening to God's voice and talking to Him. Prayer begins with seeking God for the knowledge of His will and ultimately agreeing with what He desires to do in the earth to advance His kingdom. Jesus was our perfect model for prayer. He listened for the Father's voice and only said what He heard the Father saying.

In the Greek language, "pray" is the word "*proseuchomai*" [*pros-yoo'-khom-ahee*], which is broken down into two words, "*pros*", which means towards, and "*seuchomai*", which means to wish or to pray.

By definition, our prayers are directed towards God. When we come to Him in prayer, we must line ourselves up with His will and, according to His will, ask for the things that we need each day to advance His kingdom. This is the Biblical definition of prayer. Prayer is also about giving thanks to God for all that He has done and will do. It is our opportunity to thank and worship Him.

The Holy Spirit is the Lord of your prayer life and makes intercession for you so that you know what to pray. As you come into agreement with God's Word, will and way in prayer, your prayers will be powerful and effective.

Why do I need to pray?

> Read James 5:13-18, 1 John 5:14-15

Prayer produces greater intimacy with God and advances His kingdom on Earth. Prayer releases the power of God in your life for provision, forgiveness, healing, deliverance and His perfect will. You pray in the secret place to deepen your relationship with God; in the gathering place to join with other believers in unified agreement with God; and in the market place to bring His kingdom rule into all the Earth. Cultivating a lifestyle of prayer is essential to your daily life as a believer.

How do you pray?

Read Matthew 6:6-13 and 1 Thessalonians 5:16-19

The disciples saw the fruit of Jesus' prayer life, and they wanted Him to teach them how to pray. They saw times when He prayed during the day[1], times when He prayed all night[2], and times when He prayed alone with the Father[3].

Jesus teaches a model for daily prayer that is both a pattern to follow and a prayer to be prayed. Effective prayer requires you to daily worship, intently seek the will of God in the earth, expect and receive spiritual nourishment, confess and repent of sin, forgive those who have sinned against you, and actively seek the way of righteousness and the defeat of evil.

As you pray in the secret place in your daily times with God, your intimacy with God will increase. Out of the intimacy in the secret place will flow more power in the gathering place as you pray with other believers, and in the market place as you bring His kingdom ways into the lives of those you encounter.

examine — Take 10 minutes to examine your secret place prayer time. What plan has the Lord revealed for you to follow in your times with Him? If you do not have a plan for your secret place prayer time, ask the Holy Spirit, the Lord of your prayer life, to show you when and where your prayer time with Him will be. He has a time and place for you!

express — Use the journal pages provided to write out the plan that the Lord has revealed to you regarding your secret place prayer time. Write out a prayer using the model prayer discussed in this lesson to acknowledge areas of needed growth and transformation in your daily prayer life. **Speak this prayer aloud** and engage in dynamic conversation with the Lord.

---

[1] Luke 3:21
[2] Luke 6:12
[3] Luke 5:15-16; 9:18

exercise — Make your daily secret place prayer time a priority. Listen, speak, sing and meditate on His Word. Also, make a point to be a part of corporate times of prayer that are made available.

SECTION 2:

The Study of Prayer

This inductive Bible study will help you respond in obedience to the truth of God's Word. As you look at each passage of Scripture below, *examine* what it says, *express* what it means, and consider how you will *exercise* it in your life. Use the Inductive Bible Study Guidelines at the beginning of your handbook and the worksheets provided on the next pages to help you.

examine — Read *1 John 5:14 & 15*, and write it down using the journal pages provided.

express — Now read these scriptures aloud and declare your commitment to the truth of them in your life. Use the worksheets provided to rewrite these scriptures in your own words.

exercise — Write down 2-3 action steps that you will take based on the truth of *1 John 5:14 & 15* using the journal pages provided.

Inductive Bible Study Worksheet

Inductive Bible Study Worksheet

Inductive Bible Study Worksheet

SECTION 3:

The Discussion about Prayer

Use the journal pages provided to write your response to each of these questions in preparation for a group discussion.

examine — Examine your prayer times this week. Ask the Lord to show you where your perspective on prayer has been different from what Jesus teaches in the Word as well as areas of prayerlessness in your daily life. Confess to the group what He shows you, and encourage one another with the truth about prayer according to the Bible, as discussed in this lesson.

express — Take some time to write down any obstacles and distractions that keep you from prayer in the secret place, gathering place and market place. Share these obstacles and distractions with those in your group. Ask for feedback and prayer over these things.

exercise — How will you go to the next level of intimacy with the Lord in your prayer times? Talk with the group about the next steps the Lord is leading you to take and commit yourself to rightly relating to God through times of prayer.

Marks of Maturing

These are the Marks of Maturing as someone who prays. How well do they describe you? Use the journal pages provided to write your response.

- A disciple is someone who seeks after God for the knowledge of His will and ultimately agrees to His desires by only doing and saying what He does and says.

- A disciple is someone who cultivates a lifestyle of prayer in the secret place, the gathering place and the market place in order to see God's power released in his/her life.

- A disciple is someone who has an effective, daily prayer time worshipping, seeking God's will in the earth, expecting and receiving spiritual nourishment, confessing and repenting of sin, forgiving others' sins and actively seeking the way of righteousness and the defeat of evil.

Go Further

Here are some optional readings for you as you live a lifestyle of prayer:

"To be a Christian without prayer is no more possible than to be alive without breathing." ~ Martin Luther[1]

"You can do more than pray after you have prayed; but you can never do more than pray until you have prayed." ~ A.J. Gordon[2]

"Prayer should not be regarded as a duty which must be performed, but rather as a privilege to be enjoyed, a rare delight that is always revealing some new beauty." ~ E.M. Bounds[3]

*****

---

[1] www.thinkexist.com, Martin Luther, Priest and Professor of Theology, 1483 – 1546
[2] www.christianquotes.com, A.J. Gordon, American Baptist preacher, writer, composer, and founder of Gordon College, 1836 – 1895
[3] www.christianquotes.com, Edward McKendree Bounds, Clergyman and Author, 1835-1913

Jesus gives us the pattern prayer in what is commonly known as "The Lord's Prayer." In this model of perfect prayer, He gives us a law form to be followed, and yet one to be filled in and enlarged as we may decide when we pray. The outlines and form are complete, yet it is but an outline, with many a blank, which our needs and convictions are to fill in.

Christ puts words on our lips, words which are to be uttered by holy lives. Words belong to the life of prayer. Wordless prayers are like human spirits; pure and high they may be, but too ethereal and impalpable for earthly conflicts and earthly needs and uses. We must have spirits clothed in flesh and blood, and our prayers must be likewise clothed in words to give them point and power, a local habitation, and a name.

This lesson of "The Lord's Prayer," drawn forth by the request of the disciples, "Lord, teach us to pray," has something in form and verbiage like the prayer sections of the Sermon on the Mount. It is the same great lesson of praying to "Our Father which art in Heaven," and is one of insistent importunity. No prayer lesson would be complete without it. It belongs to the first and last lessons in prayer. God's Fatherhood gives shape, value and confidence to all our praying.

In this prayer He teaches His disciples, so familiar to thousands in this day who learned it at their mother's knees in childhood, the words are so childlike that children find their instruction, edification and comfort in them as they kneel and pray. The most glowing mystic and the most careful thinker finds each his own language in these simple words of prayer. Beautiful and revered as these words are, they are our words for solace, help and learning.

He led the way in prayer that we might follow His footsteps. Matchless leader in matchless praying! Lord, teach us to pray as Thou didst Thyself pray![4]

---

[4] *The Reality of Prayer X*, Edward McKendree Bounds, Baker Books, 2004

"Forgive"

LESSON 8

SECTION 1:

A Story of Forgiveness

Read Matthew 18:21-35

Jesus' disciple Peter came to Him and said, "Lord, how often shall my brother sin against me, and I forgive him? Up to seven times?" Peter undoubtedly thought he was being quite generous in his willingness to forgive up to seven times since Jewish tradition held that three times was the limit. Jesus responded, "I do not say to you, up to seven times, but up to seventy times seven." He then told him a story that would further reveal the expected scope of forgiveness for a follower of Christ.

Jesus spoke of two men who were indebted to others. One man, indebted to a king, owed 10,000 talents. Ten thousand talents would have been 60 million days' wages, an amount impossible to repay. The king, moved with compassion over the man's plight, forgave the entire debt. The second man, indebted to the man who had been forgiven his own incredible debt, owed 100 denarii. A hundred denarii was a little over three months' wages. Rather than showing mercy and forgiving this relatively small debt, he had him thrown into prison. While he had been shown tremendous mercy and compassion, he showed none in return. When it was reported to the king what had happened, he became very angry. He roundly rebuked him and turned him over to the authorities to be beaten and jailed. Jesus declared that there would be serious consequences for not sincerely forgiving others.

The point of the story is quite clear: We have been forgiven a debt that we had no capacity to repay. Jesus, through being beaten, tortured and crucified, paid in full our debt completely and forever. We then are called to forgive others to the same degree that we have been forgiven by God the Father through Jesus the Son. Forgiveness is being willing to live with the consequences of another's sin against us and to cancel their debt to us. This enables God to continue to forgive our debts, keeping us free and clean in Christ. By God's grace, we have the capacity to choose to forgive and to keep our "ledgers" clean.

The Definition of Forgiveness

What does it mean to forgive?

> Read Luke 11:4, Colossians 1:13-14 and 1 John 1:9

Forgiveness is the cornerstone of your relationship with God. He sent His Son to die as the ultimate act of forgiveness and payment for your sin. When you confess and repent of your sin, God completely cleanses you and forgives you of your sin. He frees you from the guilt, shame and power that sin has in your life and releases you from the sin itself. Because the Lord forgives you completely, you are then able to forgive others in the same way.

In the Greek language, the word "*opheileo*" [*of-i-leh'-o*] is the idea of accruing debt, to owe, or to be under obligation. Also in the Greek language, the word "*aphiemi*" [*ah-fee-ay-mee*] is the idea of sending away, letting go, giving up a debt, keeping it no longer. Simply put, it is to take the weight off of someone's shoulders.

When you confess your sin to the Lord, He is faithful to forgive you, removing the weight of your sin. When someone has sinned against you, they are in essence indebted to you. When you forgive them, you free them from having to fulfill that obligation. Forgiveness releases them from paying what they owe to you and cancels their debt to you completely.

Why do I need to forgive?

> Read Matthew 6:14-15, Luke 6:37 and John 20:23

You forgive because God forgives and because Jesus commands it. When you confess your sins, you are able to have the power and purity of God flow through you. You are forgiven by the Lord, and then you continue to forgive others on an ongoing basis. Unforgiveness is sin to the Lord.

When you forgive, you reflect the generous, loving character of God. Forgiveness removes anything that would keep you from the free-flowing presence of the Lord in your life. Forgiveness allows you to have a deep and intimate relationship with God.

How do I forgive?

Read Matthew 18:21-35 and Mark 11:25-26

The pathway to forgiving others is by first confessing your own sin and being forgiven by the Lord. You can only truly forgive when you understand that God forgives you completely. Once you are clean before the Lord, it makes way for you to forgive others.

You forgive others by releasing them from the obligation of having to fulfill whatever "debt" they owe to you. You do not demand justice or repayment for injury and loss. You release them completely. God is the One who cleanses them of their sin.

You are called to continually forgive people of their debts to you. God never tires of forgiving us and gives us the ability to forgive others as well.

examine — Take 10 minutes to allow the Holy Spirit to search your heart and bring fresh revelation on and commitment to what it means to forgive. In light of God's forgiveness, are there specific people that you have not fully forgiven? Write down the names of those people that you are to forgive.

express — Take the list of names from the previous step and speak aloud that you forgive them, releasing them from any debt or obligation they might owe you. Speak the words out loud with faith, knowing that as you release them, you are permitting the life of Jesus to be released in your own life.

exercise — As you begin each day by coming before the Lord in the secret place, ask Him to search your heart and forgive you of your sin. Then spend time asking the Holy Spirit to reveal if there is anyone else you need to forgive. Use the steps in the Express section above to walk in full forgiveness.

SECTION 2:

The Study of Forgiveness

This inductive Bible study will help you respond in obedience to the truth of God's Word. As you look at each passage of Scripture below, *examine* what it says, *express* what it means, and consider how you will *exercise* it in your life. Use the Inductive Bible Study Guidelines at the beginning of your handbook and the worksheets provided on the next pages to help you.

examine — Read *Mark 11:25-26*, and write it down using the journal pages provided.

express — Read these scriptures aloud and declare your commitment to the truth of them in your life. Use the worksheets provided to rewrite these scriptures in your own words.

exercise — Write down 2-3 action steps that you will take based on the truth of *Mark 11:25-26* using the journal pages provided.

Inductive Bible Study Worksheet

Inductive Bible Study Worksheet

Inductive Bible Study Worksheet

SECTION 3:
The Discussion about Forgiveness

Use the journal pages provided to write your response to each of these questions in preparation for a group discussion.

examine — Ask the Holy Spirit to search your heart and mind, letting Him show you places where there is unforgiveness. What keeps you from forgiving debts of those who are indebted to you? Are you willing to forgive as Jesus said, from the heart, completely releasing people from their debt?

express — Share with the group the areas in your life where the Holy Spirit has revealed unforgiveness against someone or against the Lord. What steps will you take to be a rapid repenter and a fast forgiver?

exercise — Commit to keep a short account with people, not letting debts stack up in your heart and mind. Pray for one another for a revelation of God's forgiveness that will free you completely to forgive others as you have been forgiven.

Marks of Maturing

These are the Marks of Maturing as someone who forgives. How well do they describe you? Use the journal pages provided to write your response.

- A disciple is someone walks in complete forgiveness from the Lord and extends complete forgiveness to others.

- A disciple is someone who has the power and purity of God in their lives as a result of being forgiven and forgiving others.

- A disciple is someone who does not demand justice or repayment for injury or loss, but instead releases others completely from any obligation.

Go Further

Here are some optional readings for you as you live a lifestyle of forgiveness:

"He who cannot forgive others destroys the bridge over which he himself must pass." ~ George Herbert[1]

"To forgive is to set a prisoner free and discover that the prisoner was you." ~Lewis B. Smedes[2]

---

[1] www.christianquotes.com, George Herbert, Anglican Priest, 1593 – 1633

[2] www.thinkexist.com, Lewis B. Smedes, Christian Author and Professor of Theology and Ethics, 1921 – 2002

The victim may say, "I can't forgive these people. You don't now how bad they hurt me." The problem is, they are still hurting you. How do you stop the pain? Forgiveness is what sets us free from the past. What is to be gained in forgiving is freedom. You don't heal in order to forgive. You forgive in order to heal. Forgiveness is to set a captive free and then to realize you were the captive. You don't forgive others for their sake; you do it for your sake. Those you need to forgive may never be aware of your choice to let them off your hook. Forgiveness is the fragrance that is left on the heel that crushed the violet.[3]

"To be a Christian means to forgive the inexcusable, because God has forgiven the inexcusable in you." ~ C.S. Lewis[4]

---

[3] *Victory Over The Darkness*, Neil T. Anderson, Regal Publishing, Ventura CA, 2000, p. 192
[4] *www.christianquotes.com*, Clive Staples Lewis, Novelist/Christian Apologist, 1898 1963

"Give" — LESSON 9

SECTION 1:

A Story of Giving

Read Malachi 1:6-8, 3:8-12

There was a season in Judah's history when they had fallen into spiritual indifference. They were offering blemished sacrifices and holding back in the releasing of tithes and offerings. According to Malachi, it revealed what was in the people's hearts: a lack of love and honor for God. God called them to give an account for why they were not honoring Him in their giving. He, through Malachi, said to them, "A son honors his father, and his servant his master. If then I am the Father, where is my honor? And if I am a Master, where is my reverence?" Additionally, God accused the people of robbing Him. The people were dumbfounded. "How have we robbed you?" they wanted to know. God told them that they had robbed Him by withholding their tithes (a tenth of their income) and by not giving generous offerings to support the work of serving people in need.

Though the people had been disrespectful and disobedient in not giving the best of their lives and resources to God, He promised them that if they would give as He commanded, He would bless and prosper them abundantly. He also told them that He would protect and preserve their possessions. Malachi prophesied that if the people would honor and love God fully, He would pour out the limitless supply of heaven. God's desire was to live in a covenantal union with His people, blessing them as they honored Him with their devotion to Him in everything.

The practice of giving tithes and offerings is God's plan for us to enter into a financial covenant with Him. It reveals our commitment to love and honor God with the financial resources He entrusts to us. As we give as commanded, we will reap both spiritual and financial benefits from God. When we give a tenth of our income and release generous offerings for various ministry needs, we can be sure that God will "pour out for us such blessing that there will not be room enough to contain it."

The Definition of Give

What does it mean to give?

Read Genesis 14:18-20 and Deuteronomy 14:22-26

The Lord calls you to steward the possessions He entrusts to you, which includes money. You give money in the form of tithes, offerings and alms. Giving of the finances that the Lord has blessed you with is a statement of honor, trust and love for Him.

In the Greek language, to tithe is the word *"dekatos"* [*dek'-at-os*], which means a tenth, or give the tenth part. To give offerings is the word *"didomi"* [*did'-o-mee*] which means to offer or give something to someone. And to give alms is the word *"eleemosyne"* [*e-le-ā-mo-sü'-nā*], which means a donation to the poor.

Tithing predates the Law. The first humans tithed[1], and our father of faith Abraham, tithed as well. It is the command of the Lord to give to Him a tenth of the first fruits of all that you have. "The earth is the LORD's, and all its fullness." It all belongs to Him! Tithes are a tenth of your first fruits—paying 10 percent to the Lord before you pay anything else.

Offerings and alms are those gifts that God would prompt you to give through the leading of the Holy Spirit. Offerings are monies given to the church for the purpose of missions and special offerings for specific needs. They are financial gifts that are above and beyond the tithe. Alms are monies given to the poor. Throughout the Bible, there are numerous examples of giving to the poor and how it brings God's pleasure and blessing on your life.

Why do I give?

Read Malachi 3:8-12 and Matthew 6:19-33

Malachi tells you that if you honor the Lord with the paying of your tithes, He will "open the windows of heaven and pour out for you such a blessing" and that He will "rebuke the devourer." Finally, He says, "Nor shall the vine fail to bear fruit." Though the main currency of the Israelites was produce and livestock, the principle is the same with money. The Lord will bless you and the finances He entrusts to you, and He will bring great revelation to you if you honor and trust Him by paying your tithes and giving offerings and alms.

---

[1] Genesis 4
[2] Psalm 24:1

Jesus said that you should lay up treasures in heaven not on earth, for those on earth will eventually be destroyed or even stolen. He says, "For where your treasure is, there your heart will be also." He concludes by saying that if you seek His kingdom first, all the things you need will be added to you. You can trust Him. You see in the Bible that no one in the early church lacked because people gave generously of all that they had and did not hold on to money or possessions as their own.

How do I give?

Read 2 Corinthians 9:6-15 and Acts 2:44-45, 4:32-37

Speaking of an offering to help the poor of Jerusalem, Paul encouraged the believers at Corinth to give offerings "...as he purposes in his heart,"[4] to give; and to give with a cheerful heart, because "...God loves a cheerful giver." You give out of a cheerful heart. You give out of a thankful heart. You give out of a trusting heart, knowing, "...my God shall supply all your needs according to His riches in glory by Christ Jesus."[3]

Also, as you read in the book of Acts and in other New Testament writings, people of the New Testament were encouraged to give to the work of ministry through tithes, offerings and alms. If you are to return and reform to the ways God wants you to live and have the blessings you read about in the Bible, you need to give generously like the early church. Giving to the poor and giving to missions was a regular part of church life. You must recognize that you are really giving to the Lord when you give financially. Tithing and giving are acts of worship to the Lord.

examine — Take a few minutes to examine your heart to see if your uses of the monies and resources God has entrusted to you reflect His ownership of all things, as well as His commands and desires for how those resources should be used.

exercise — All of us have been convicted by the Holy Spirit in regards to a lack of generosity at times. Take a few moments to declare that you understand that everything belongs to the Lord, and that you will respond in obedience and generosity as He brings opportunities before you to give.

---

[3] 2 Corinthians 9:7

express — Take each opportunity that is presented to you to give to the kingdom, whether through paying your tithe or giving offerings or alms; and then see His faithfulness to His word open the windows of heaven to bless you.

SECTION 2:

The Study of Giving

This inductive Bible study will help you respond in obedience to the truth of God's Word. As you look at each passage of Scripture below, *examine* what it says, *express* what it means, and consider how you will *exercise* it in your life. Use the Inductive Bible Study Guidelines at the beginning of your handbook and the worksheets provided on the next pages to help you.

examine — Read *Malachi 3:10-12*, and write it down using the journal pages provided.

exercise — Read these scriptures aloud and declare your commitment to the truth of them in your life. Use the worksheets provided to rewrite these scriptures in your own words.

express — Write down 2-3 action steps that you will take based on the truth of *Malachi 3:10-12* using the journal pages provided.

Inductive Bible Study Worksheet

examine

Inductive Bible Study Worksheet

Inductive Bible Study Worksheet

SECTION 3:

The Discussion about Giving

Use the journal pages provided to write your response to each of these questions in preparation for a group discussion.

examine — How have you seen God's faithfulness as you have been obedient to tithe, give offerings and alms? Share an example of God's provision in your life.

express — During economic challenges, has your perspective on material things shifted? Are you willing to give up your luxuries so that others are able to have their necessities? Be specific.

exercise — What changes do you need to make in your life in order for God's kingdom to be advanced through the sowing of your finances? Remember, everything you have is really God's.

Marks of Maturing

These are the Marks of Maturing as someone who gives. How well do they describe you? Use the journal pages provided to write your response.

- A disciple is someone who regularly pays tithes and gives offerings and alms.

- A disciple is someone who gives generously, not holding onto money or possessions as their own.

- A disciple is someone who gives with a cheerful, thankful and trusting heart.

Go Further

Here are some optional readings for you as you live a lifestyle of giving:

"Jesus Christ said more about money than about any other single thing because, when it comes to a man's real nature, money is of first importance. Money is an exact index to a man's true character. All through Scripture there is an intimate correlation between the development of a man's character and how he handles his money." ~ Richard C. Halverson[12]

"Worship is giving God the best that He has given you. Be careful what you do with the best you have. Whenever you get a blessing from God, give it back to Him as a love gift. Take time to meditate before God and offer the blessing back to Him in a deliberate act of worship. If you hoard a thing for yourself, it will turn into spiritual dry rot, as the manna did when it was hoarded. God will never let you hold a spiritual thing for yourself; it has to be given back to Him that He may make it a blessing to others." ~ Oswald Chambers[5]

---

[12] *www.dailychristianquote.com*, Richard C. Halverson, Presbyterian Minister, 1916 – 1995

[5] *My Utmost For His Highest*, Oswald Chambers, Dodd Mead and Company, New York, NY, 1935

"God has given us two hands -- one to receive with and the other to give with. We are not cisterns made for hoarding; we are channels made for giving." ~ Billy Graham[6]

"Much has been said about giving a tenth of one's income to the Lord. I think that is a Christian duty which none should, for a moment, question." ~ C.H. Spurgeon[7]

---

[6] *www.dailychristianquote.com*, Billy Graham, Evangelical Christian Evangelist, 1918–

[7] "A Cheerful Giver Is Beloved Of God", Sermon #835, C. H. Spurgeon, British Baptist Preacher, 1834 – 1892

"Serve"

LESSON 10

SECTION 1:

A Story of Serving

Read John 13:1-17

Shortly before Jesus' crucifixion, He celebrated the Passover with His disciples. Passover was the Jewish feast that commemorated God delivering Israel from their slavery in Egypt. Jesus used this occasion to teach His disciples a very important lesson on serving others in His name. After they had finished supper, Jesus took a basin filled with water and a towel and began to wash the feet of His disciples. To His followers, this must have been quite a remarkable thing. The washing of feet was typically a lowly servant's job. Jesus, as the host of this dinner, was in no way the one who "should" have been doing such an undignified and dirty job. And beyond that, He was their Teacher and their Lord. Simon Peter was astounded by what was happening, and said, "Lord are you washing my feet?" Jesus responded to Peter by saying, "What I am doing you do not understand now, but you will know after this." Peter protested, evidently embarrassed by the notion of His Lord washing feet, saying, "You shall never wash my feet!" Jesus answered him with these words: "If I do not wash you, you have no part with Me." Jesus, by washing Peter's feet, was using a prophetic symbol for the spiritual cleansing His death would provide, as well as a practical example of how he and his fellow disciples were to serve one another and the world. After Jesus finished, He went on to tell these men, "I have given you an example, that you should do as I have done to you." Jesus modeled what true servanthood is—true servanthood is taking the lowest place to meet the greatest need.

For each of us, there is a need to passionately and joyfully obey Christ's command to serve. Our world is filled with great need; Jesus calls us to meet it. Jesus said in Mark 10:45, "For even the Son of Man did not come to be served, but to serve, and to give His life a ransom for many." Jesus calls us to recognize that true greatness in life is found in serving Him and others.

The Definition of Serving

What does it mean to serve?

> Read Luke 4:8, Luke 17:8-10 and Romans 7:6

When you serve God, you worship Him and give Him the service that He deserves. You live according to His plans and desires for your life and not according to your preferences. God gives you the ability to help fill the needs of others. When you serve others, it is an act of worship to God.

The New Testament uses two Greek words for the word "serve." "*Latreuo*" means to worship, minister to and to worship God in the manner that He has prescribed. "*Diakoneo*" is always used in service to the fellow man. It is to be an attendant, to wait upon, to minister to someone and to be a servant. You are to consider yourself as a servant. It is not just something you do, it is who you are.

You minister to people when you serve them by doing for them what they can't do for themselves. If you are a leader, you must see yourself as Jesus did. A leader is a servant to those they lead. See yourself as someone who is to meet needs and ministers and speaks the truth in love to people. Servants are motivated by love for the Lord and their fellow man.

Why do I serve?

> Read Mark 10:45, Matthew 20:28 and John 13:13-17

The Bible calls you to serve God. Inherent in that call is the call to serve you fellow man. Jesus, your Savior and Lord, did not see Himself as just th Savior of all but as a servant to all mankind. He gave a clear example of this when He was speaking to His disciples in John 13. He, being the Master washed His disciples' feet. If you are to obey Him fully and live as he lived you are called to serve those around you. To serve those He calls you t serve is an act of worship and obedience to your Lord Jesus.

How do I serve?

Read 2 Timothy 1:3, Galatians 5:13, Hebrews 12:28 and Philippians 2:1-8

You are to serve with love being your primary motivation. You cannot, and must not, serve out of selfish ambition ("promote me") or self-righteousness ("look at me"). You are to have the same attitude as your Lord Jesus, which is an attitude of humility and the mindset of a servant. You must have in mind that you do not live to be served but to serve the needs of others. You must consider yourself a servant and slave of Jesus Christ.

examine — Take 10 minutes to pray and ask the Lord to show you where you might be operating according to your own preferences rather than humbly serving God in His plans and purposes. Ask the Holy Spirit to examine your motivations for serving others.

express — Acknowledge each area in your life where your motives are not completely pure or you are walking in your preferences. Take time to confess this as sin and repent before God. Ask the Lord to cleanse you of any attitudes of self-promotion or self-righteousness.

exercise — Make a fresh commitment to serve God with love as your primary motivation. Ask for a fresh anointing of the Holy Spirit to show you secret ways to serve, knowing that God will reward what you do secretly in the open. As you go through each day, abide in God's presence and favor as you serve Him joyfully by serving others.

SECTION 2:

The Study of Serving

This inductive Bible study will help you respond in obedience to the truth of God's Word. As you look at each passage of Scripture below, *examine* what it says, *express* what it means, and consider how you will *exercise* it in your life. Use the Inductive Bible Study Guidelines at the beginning of your handbook and the worksheets provided on the next pages to help you.

examine — Read *Philippians 2:5-8,* and write it down using the journal pages provided.

express — Read these scriptures aloud and declare your commitment to the truth of them in your life. Use the worksheets provided to rewrite these scriptures in your own words.

exercise — Write down 2-3 action steps that you will take based on the truth of *Philippians 2:5-8* using the journal pages provided.

Inductive Bible Study Worksheet

Inductive Bible Study Worksheet

Inductive Bible Study Worksheet

SECTION 3:

The Discussion about Serving

Use the journal pages provided to write your response to each of these questions in preparation for a group discussion.

examine — Ask the Holy Spirit to speak to you now about a specific area of your life where you have not been serving well, been serving with wrongful motivations, or been grudgingly serving. What are those areas? What will you do to better walk with a servant heart, placing others first?

express — Share with the group a time where you served out of obedience to the Lord. How did it feel? How did it impact you and those you served? Did you seek honor for your good deed, or did you seek to bring honor to the Lord? Ask the Holy Spirit to show you an area or someone right now where He wants you to serve and share that person/situation with the group.

exercise — Commit to the Lord that you will obey His commandment to serve Him and others. What are the action steps you need to take to walk in obedience to the area(s) or people He has shown you to serve? Remember, by serving others you are serving the Lord!

Marks of Maturing

These are the Marks of Maturing as someone who serves. How well do they describe you? Use the journal pages provided to write your response.

- A disciple is someone who lives according to God's plans and purposes as they serve, not according to their preferences.

- A disciple is someone who serves obediently without complaint.

- A disciple is someone who serves with love as their primary motivation, without selfish ambition or self-righteousness.

Go Further

Here are some optional readings for you as you live a lifestyle of serving:

"We must be silent before we can listen. We must listen before we can learn. We must learn before we can prepare. We must prepare before we can serve. We must serve before we can lead." ~ William Arthur Ward[1]

****

"The authority by which the Christian leader leads is not power but love, not force but example, not coercion but reasoned persuasion. Leaders have power, but power is safe only in the hands of those who humble themselves to serve." ~ John Stott[2]

****

"Spirit filled souls are ablaze for God. They love with a love that glows. They serve with a faith that kindles. They serve with a devotion that consumes. They hate sin with fierceness that burns. They rejoice with a joy that radiates. Love is perfected in the fire of God." ~ Samuel Chadwick[3]

****

---

[1] www.thinkexist.com, William Arthur Ward, Author, 1921 – 1994
[2] www.christianquotes.com, John Stott, Anglican Clergyman, 1921–
[3] www.christianquotes.com, Samuel Chadwick, Methodist Minister, 1860 – 1932

Ephesians 6:6-8 (The Message Bible)

Servants, respectfully obey your earthly masters but always with an eye to obeying the real master, Christ. Don't just do what you have to do to get by but work heartily, as Christ's servants doing what God wants you to do. And work with a smile on your face, always keeping in mind that no matter who happens to be giving the orders, you're really serving God. Good work will get you good pay from the Master, regardless of whether you are slave or free.

****

Colossians 3:23-24 (The Message Bible)

Servants, do what you're told by your earthly masters. And don't just do the minimum that will get you by. Do your best. Work from the heart for your real Master, for God, confident that you'll get paid in full when you come into your inheritance. Keep in mind always that the ultimate Master you're serving is Christ. The sullen servant who does shoddy work will be held responsible. Being a follower of Jesus doesn't cover up bad work.

"Preach"	LESSON 11

SECTION 1:

A Story About Preaching

Read Acts 2:1-41

Right before He ascended to heaven, Jesus told His disciples that, after receiving the power of the Holy Spirit, they would be "witnesses" of and for Him in both word and deed. Jesus promised them that they would have everything they needed to preach the gospel and to demonstrate its power fully.

On the Day of Pentecost, fifty days after Passover, God's Spirit was poured out in a marvelous and miraculous way. One hundred and twenty people were filled with the Holy Spirit and began to speak in languages they had never learned. They spilled out into the street as a redemptive force, ready to bring lost people to the Savior, Jesus Christ. Peter became the spokesman for the group and began to preach—or proclaim with passion and power—the good news of salvation through Christ. He spoke of God's plan to send His Son to live as a man in sinless perfection, reveal God's plan of salvation, be crucified for the sins of mankind, ascend to the Father and pour out God's transformational life on anyone who would believe on Him. The people who were listening were "cut to the heart," convicted by the Holy Spirit of their sinfulness as well as their need to respond to this dramatic message. They all said, "Men and brethren, what shall we do?" Peter responded, "Repent, and let every one of you be baptized in the name of Jesus Christ for the remission of sins; and you shall receive the gift of the Holy Spirit." That day, 3000 people responded to the preaching of the gospel and were baptized in water and with the Holy Spirit.

Like Peter of old, every one of Jesus' followers is called to preach and proclaim the good news of Christ's love and power. Whether we are addressing a group, or simply sharing with an individual, we are called to preach. God has given us the truth of His Word and the power of the Holy Spirit to effectively bring lost people to the living Lord Jesus. We must speak and not be silent.

The Definition of Preaching

What does it mean to preach?

> Read 2 Corinthians 4:5 and Isaiah 61:1

When it comes to preaching, actions are important, but words are necessary. To preach the gospel is to proclaim the good news of salvation and reconciliation that comes through the person and work of Jesus Christ. You, as a redeemed person, have a message of hope to preach to people all over the world who need it.

Both the Hebrew and Greek words used in the Bible have the undeniable sense of speaking. The Hebrew word "*qara*" [*ka-ra*] means to call, to call out, to recite, to read, to cry out, to proclaim. The Greek word "*karusso*" [*ka-russo*], means to be a herald, or to proclaim openly. The other Greek word used for preach is "*euangelizo*" [*eu-an-ge-lizo*], which means to bring a message, or to announce good news.

As a believer, you have good news to share with people—God has a purpose and meaning for your life; you fit into a grand plan and can have free eternal life through God's Son. To preach the good news of Jesus Christ must involve words not just actions.

Why should I preach?

> Read Mark 16:15, Luke 4:18 and Acts 14:15

The simple answer to why you should preach the gospel is that your Lord Jesus commands you to do so in the Bible. You are to be a bearer of His good news, the news of reconciliation, salvation and eternal life—declaring the kingdom of God and the power of God. When you preach the gospel, you are revealing to people the most important truth in life—that God loves them and has done everything for them to be reconciled to Him through His son, Jesus, so that their lives will bring glory to God and their words would preach this same message of hope to others.

People are dying daily and going to the very real place called hell because they have not been told about the life they could have in Jesus. Hell is a place of continual death and separation from God. They will never return or get set free, they are there for eternity. Because of this reality, you must be about the Father's business, preaching the gospel to reveal the truth to people in order to redeem and set them free from sin and eternal death.

How do I preach?

Read Acts 17:3, Romans 10:15 and Philippians 3:3-14

You preach the gospel by telling God's story. You tell of God creating the universe and everything in it—the plants and animals and, finally, human beings. He created all people to have an intimate, loving relationship with Him, with each other and with all of creation. But man decided to go His own way and rebelled against God by disobeying. Sin entered the picture and caused a permanent breaking of all those relationships, ultimately leading to death and eternal separation from God for mankind. In His infinite love and mercy, God had a plan. That plan was Jesus.

When you preach, you tell of His life, death and resurrection and explain that only through repenting of your sin and placing your faith in Jesus as Savior and Lord, can those broken relationships be restored and the gift of eternal life with God can be received. You tell that Jesus took all sin on His back and experienced the consequences of all your guilt so that you might experience the freedom from guilt, shame and death and enjoy all the good things of God forever.

When you preach, you also tell your story. As a believer, you have a testimony of God's saving grace and goodness in your life. When you tell this kind of story, it is a testimony of the truth of His great love and power in your life. You tell of what He is doing in your life today and of His promises for tomorrow.

When you preach, you can trust the Holy Spirit to convict and woo people to Himself. The work of salvation is His work; yours is to preach the gospel.

examine — Take 10 minutes to let the Holy Spirit show you where you have had opportunities to "preach the gospel" that you have missed. Whether you held back from speaking because of a fear of man, fear of rejection, not feeling that you knew enough, or any other reason, the truth is that the Holy Spirit was present to give you the right words. Repent and ask the Lord to forgive you and fill you with a new capacity to speak boldly.

express — Take time to practice speaking the gospel to yourself and other believers, and allow the Holy Spirit to train and equip you as well as give you boldness. Get used to hearing yourself preaching the gospel.

exercise — Find an opportunity each day to direct a conversation to the subject of Jesus, who He is and what He has done for you. Remember you cannot lose! If you are rejected and mocked, the Bible calls you "blessed"; if you are heard and received, you are partnering with the Holy Spirit in bringing salvation into someone's life.

SECTION 2:

The Study of Preaching

This inductive Bible study will help you respond in obedience to the truth of God's Word. As you look at each passage of Scripture below, *examine* what it says, *express* what it means, and consider how you will *exercise* it in your life. Use the Inductive Bible Study Guidelines at the beginning of your handbook and the worksheets provided on the next pages to help you.

examine — Read *Romans 10:13-15*, and write it down using the journal pages provided.

express — Read these scriptures aloud and declare your commitment to the truth of them in your life. Use the worksheet provided to rewrite these scriptures in your own words.

exercise — Write down 2-3 action steps that you will take based on the truth of *Romans 10:13-15* using the journal pages provided.

Inductive Bible Study Worksheet

Inductive Bible Study Worksheet

Inductive Bible Study Worksheet

exercise

SECTION 3:

The Discussion about Preaching

Use the journal pages provided to write your response to each of these questions in preparation for a group discussion.

examine — What platforms has God provided for you to preach to others about the saving power of Jesus Christ? What are places that you visit frequently (such as the gym or the grocery store)? Are you using every opportunity to share the gospel with others?

express — What are your main obstacles in preaching Christ to others? Are you concerned that you will offend or be rejected by others? Do you want your life to do the talking so you haven't used words to share with others about Jesus?

exercise — What changes do you need to make in your life in order for His gospel to be preached on a daily basis? What specific ideas is the Holy Spirit giving you to become more focused in preaching the gospel to others?

Marks of Maturing

These are the Marks of Maturing of someone who preaches. How well do they describe you? Use the journal pages provided to write your response.

- A disciple is someone who preaches the good news of Jesus Christ with their words, not just their actions.

- A disciple is someone who understands the reality of hell, and takes every opportunity to preach the truth of salvation and reconciliation through the person and work of Jesus Christ.

- A disciple is someone who tells Jesus' story and their own story, as a testimony of the truth of God's great love and power.

Go Further

Here are some optional readings for you as you walk in a lifestyle of preaching the gospel:

"The motto of all true servants of God must be, 'We preach Christ; and Him crucified.' A sermon without Christ in it is like a loaf of bread without any flour in it. No Christ in your sermon, sir? Then go home, and never preach again until you have something worth preaching." ~ Charles Spurgeon[1]

****

"The Great Commission is not an option to be considered; it is a command to be obeyed." ~ Hudson Taylor[2]

****

"Our business is to present the Christian faith clothed in modern terms, not to propagate modern thought clothed in Christian terms. Confusion here is fatal." ~ J. I. Packer[3]

---

[1] *Sermon #2899* (7/9/1876), Charles Haddon Spurgeon, Baptist Pastor, 1834 - 1992
[2] *www.christian-quotes.ochristian.com*, Hudson Taylor, British Protestant Christian Minister, 1832-1905
[3] *www.christian-quotes.ochristian.com*, J.I. Packer, Christian Theologian, 1926–

****

"Evangelism is not salesmanship. It is not urging people, pressing them coercing them, overwhelming them, or subduing them. Evangelism is telling a message. Evangelism is reporting good news." ~ Richard C. Halverson[4]

****

"Evangelism is not a professional job for a few trained men, but is instead the unrelenting responsibility of every person who belongs to the company of Jesus." ~ Elton Trueblood[6]

****

"It is not our business to make the message acceptable, but to make it available. We are not to see that they like it, but that they get it." ~ Dr. Vance Havner[7]

****

I can't impress this on you too strongly. God is looking over your shoulder Christ himself is the Judge, with the final say on everyone, living and dead He is about to break into the open with his rule, so proclaim the Message with intensity; keep on your watch. Challenge, warn, and urge your people. Don ever quit. Just keep it simple. You're going to find that there will be time when people will have no stomach for solid teaching, but will fill up on spiritual junk food—catchy opinions that tickle their fancy. They'll turn their backs on truth and chase mirages. But you—keep your eye on what you're doing; accept the hard times along with the good; keep the Message alive; do a thorough job as God's servant.[8]

---

[4] *www.dailychristianquote.com,* Richard C. Halverson, Presbyterian Minister, 1916 - 1995
[6] *www.bezeugen.org,* Elton Trueblood, American Quaker Author and Theologian, 1900-1994
[7] *www.bezeugen.org,* Dr. Vance Havner, Revivalist and Author, 1901 – 1986
[8] *The Message Bible,* 2 Timothy 4:1-3

"Abide"

LESSON 12

SECTION 1:

A Story of Abiding

Read John 15:4-11 and Acts 2:42-47

One of the last commands Jesus gave His disciples was for them to abide in Him. He told them that, in the same way the branch of a grapevine had to remain continually attached to the vine in order to receive physical life and bear physical fruit, so they had to remain in constant fellowship with Christ in order to receive spiritual life and bear spiritual fruit. He was revealing to His followers that fellowship with Him was the key to maximum spiritual fruitfulness. Additionally, Jesus told them that if they continued in ongoing intimacy with Him, which is the essence of abiding, they would be filled with the fullness of Christ's joy.

In the congregational life of the early church, we see a beautiful example of authentic abiding in Christ. We see a people deeply in love with Jesus who were living moment by moment in His presence and power—a people filled with the joy of the Lord, seeing His life manifested in and through them. They were steadfast in their commitment to the Word, to fellowship with Christ and one another, to living in unity as the Body of Christ and seeking God's will in worship and prayer. The Spirit of Christ was leading a newly redeemed people into a spirit of generosity, willing to share with whomever had need. These early Christians were walking in a spirit of daily worship, sharing meals together from house to house in the name of the Lord. And as they lived out their newfound faith in Christ, they did so with joy and gladness, simply and totally devoted to Jesus. As a result of their faith and devotion, the fruit of signs and wonders was being born. The Lord Jesus was adding new converts to His church day by day.

This is what abiding in Christ meant to them and what abiding in Christ should mean to us—being true believers who live in an unbroken union with our Savior, producing rich and redemptive fruit each and every day.

The Definition of Abiding

What does it mean to abide?

> Read John 15:1-4 and John 14:26

To abide means to dwell in or stand in something continually. To abide in Christ means that you remain in His presence, continually focused on Him and what He is saying to you.

The Greek word used in John 15 for abide is the word "*meno*" [*men'-o*], which means to stay in a given place, state, relation or expectancy; to continue; to dwell; to endure; to be present; to remain; to stand firm or steadfast; to tarry or to remain under.

The picture that the Lord gives us is that of a grapevine and its branches. The Lord's life, by His Spirit, is flowing through you, and He is also the One who leads you on a moment-by-moment basis through His Spirit. Whether you are by yourself, with others in your community, or in the marketplace, you are in submission to the leading of the Holy Spirit who is speaking to and leading you. You will hear His voice and sense His leading as you daily abide in Him.

When you are thinking, speaking and doing what Jesus would, you are abiding in Him. When you are being led by the Spirit and not by your preferences, you are abiding in Jesus.

Why do I need to abide?

> Read John 15:5-8

Your life depends on Jesus. Just as a branch has no life unless it is attached closely and consistently to the vine, you have no life unless you are connected on a daily basis to Christ. If you are to truly live the life He has for you, you must abide and remain in Him throughout the day. Your strength fails; His does not. Your wisdom runs out; His does not. Your love ends; His does not. He is the Source of all that you need.

Jesus provides His Spirit who leads and guides you, comforts you, and helps you in your time of need. When you abide in Him, you are full of His Spirit who is ready at your point of need. You are able to determine, pray and do according to His perfect will, and will bear great fruit in life as you abide in Him.

How do I abide?

Read Proverbs 3:5-10, John 14:16-18 and 1 John 2:3-11

Abiding in the Lord starts in the secret place. This is the time where you connect one-on-One with your heavenly Father, the Lord Jesus and the Holy Spirit. Giving Him the first fruits of your day is important, because when you begin focused on Him and His ability, you will then be more able to abide in Him consistently throughout the day. The key to abiding is to daily keep your focus on Jesus and what He is saying to you through His Holy Spirit, putting Him first in all that you do.

When you need wisdom, ask in faith. He will provide wisdom for anything that comes your way. When you need His love, grace, peace and joy, just ask Him. He is always with you. He will never leave or forsake you.

Spend time daily in the Word, speak out loud to the Lord in your secret place, and then pray throughout the day. Remain closely connected to Him as you learn to know His voice and do His will.

examine — Take 10 minutes to stop and listen to the Holy Spirit. Are you abiding in His presence? Do you tend to drift away from His presence at certain points of the day? What takes your attention away from Him?

express — Ask the Holy Spirit to show you a new way to live, daily abiding in the Lord. There may be times in the day that you are vulnerable to the enemy's distractions and temptations. Take time to write down places of vulnerability as well as the Holy Spirit's strategy to help you abide.

exercise — Make a fresh commitment to abide in the presence and power of Jesus. Take time to pray out loud against past patterns of sin that cause you to disconnect from Jesus. Prepare your mind for a new way to live constantly connected to Jesus. Declare your complete dependence on Him.

SECTION 2:

The Study of Abiding

This inductive Bible study will help you respond in obedience to the truth of God's Word. As you look at each passage of Scripture below, *examine* what it says, *express* what it means, and consider how you will *exercise* it in your life. Use the Inductive Bible Study Guidelines at the beginning of your handbook and the worksheets provided on the next pages to help you.

examine — Read *John 15:1-11*, and write it down using the journal pages provided.

express — Read these scriptures aloud and declare your commitment to the truth of them in your life. Use the worksheet provided to rewrite these scriptures in your own words.

exercise — Write down 2-3 action steps that you will take based on the truth of *John 15:1-11* using the journal pages provided.

Inductive Bible Study Worksheet

Inductive Bible Study Worksheet

Inductive Bible Study Worksheet

SECTION 3:

The Discussion about Abiding

Use the journal pages provided to write your response to each of these questions in preparation for a group discussion.

examine — Compare and contrast specific times in your life when you have seen the result of abiding--and not abiding--in the Lord. Share the differences with the group.

express — Do you believe that your very life depends on abiding in the Lord? Share with the group the obstacles and challenges you face in fully abiding.

exercise — Commit to the Lord that you will abide in Him moment-by-moment, day-by-day. What steps will you specifically take in order to fully abide, overcoming every obstacle and challenge? Share these with the group.

Marks of Maturing

These are the Marks of Maturing as someone who abides. How well do they describe you? Use the journal pages provided to write your response.

- A disciple is someone who thinks, speaks and does what Jesus would, being led daily by the Holy Spirit instead of his or her own preferences.

- A disciple is someone who bears great fruit as a result of determining, praying and doing according to the Lord's will every day.

- A disciple is someone who remains focused daily on Jesus and what He is saying, putting Him first in all he or she does.

Go Further

Here are some optional readings for you as you abide in the Lord:

"The connection between the vine and the branch is a living one. No external, temporary union will suffice; no work of man can effect it: the branch, whether an original or an engrafted one, is such only by the Creator's own work, in virtue of which the life, the sap, the fatness, and the fruitfulness of the vine communicate themselves to the branch. And just so it is with the believer too." ~ Andrew Murray[1]

* * * * *

"Every thing that a man leans upon but God, will be a dart that will certainly pierce his heart through and through. He who leans only upon Christ, lives the highest, choicest, safest, and sweetest life." ~ Thomas Brooks[2]

"Before one can walk as Christ walked, and talk as He talked, he must first

---

[1] *www.theoldtimegospel.org*, Andrew Murray, South African Writer, Teacher and Christian Pastor, 1828 – 1917
[2] *www.christian-resources-today.com*, Thomas Brooks, British Politician and Member of Parliament, 1880 – 1958

begin to think as Christ thought." ~ A.A. Allen[3]

* * * * *

This is how we know we're living steadily and deeply in him, and he in us: He's given us life from his life, from his very own Spirit. Also, we've seen for ourselves and continue to state openly that the Father sent his Son as Savior of the world. Everyone who confesses that Jesus is God's Son participates continuously in an intimate relationship with God. We know it so well, we've embraced it heart and soul, this love that comes from God. ~ 1 John 4:13-16[4]

---

[3] *www.tentamker.org*, A.A. Allen, Pentecostal Evangelist, 1911 – 1970
[4] *The Message Bible*, 1 John 4:13-16

disciple's
HANDBOOK

Made in the USA
Lexington, KY
21 September 2018